A MAN MADE OF STRAW

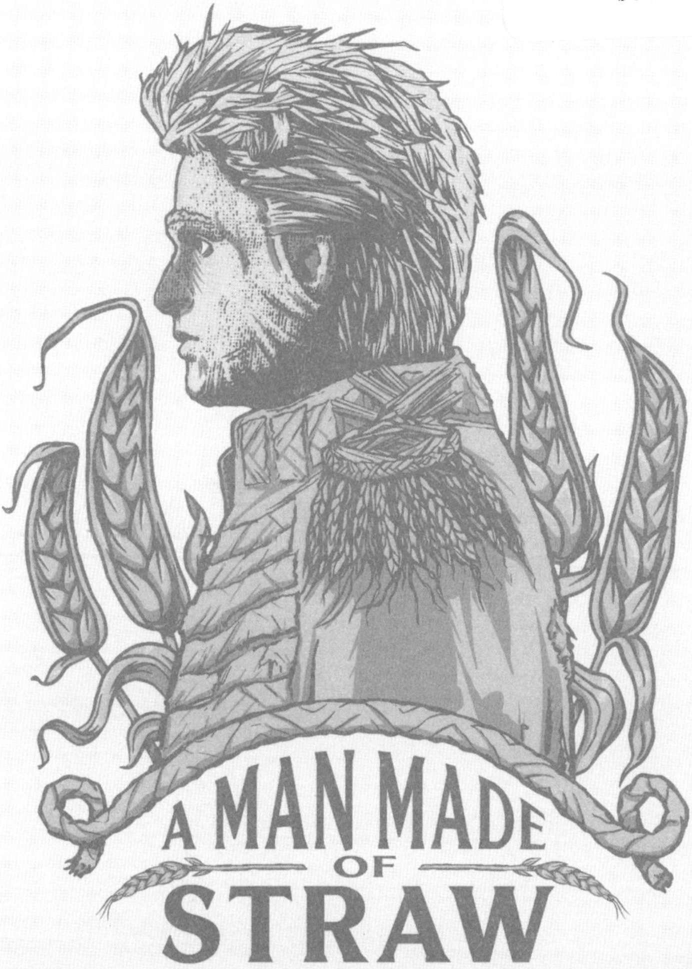

PROPERTY OF

____

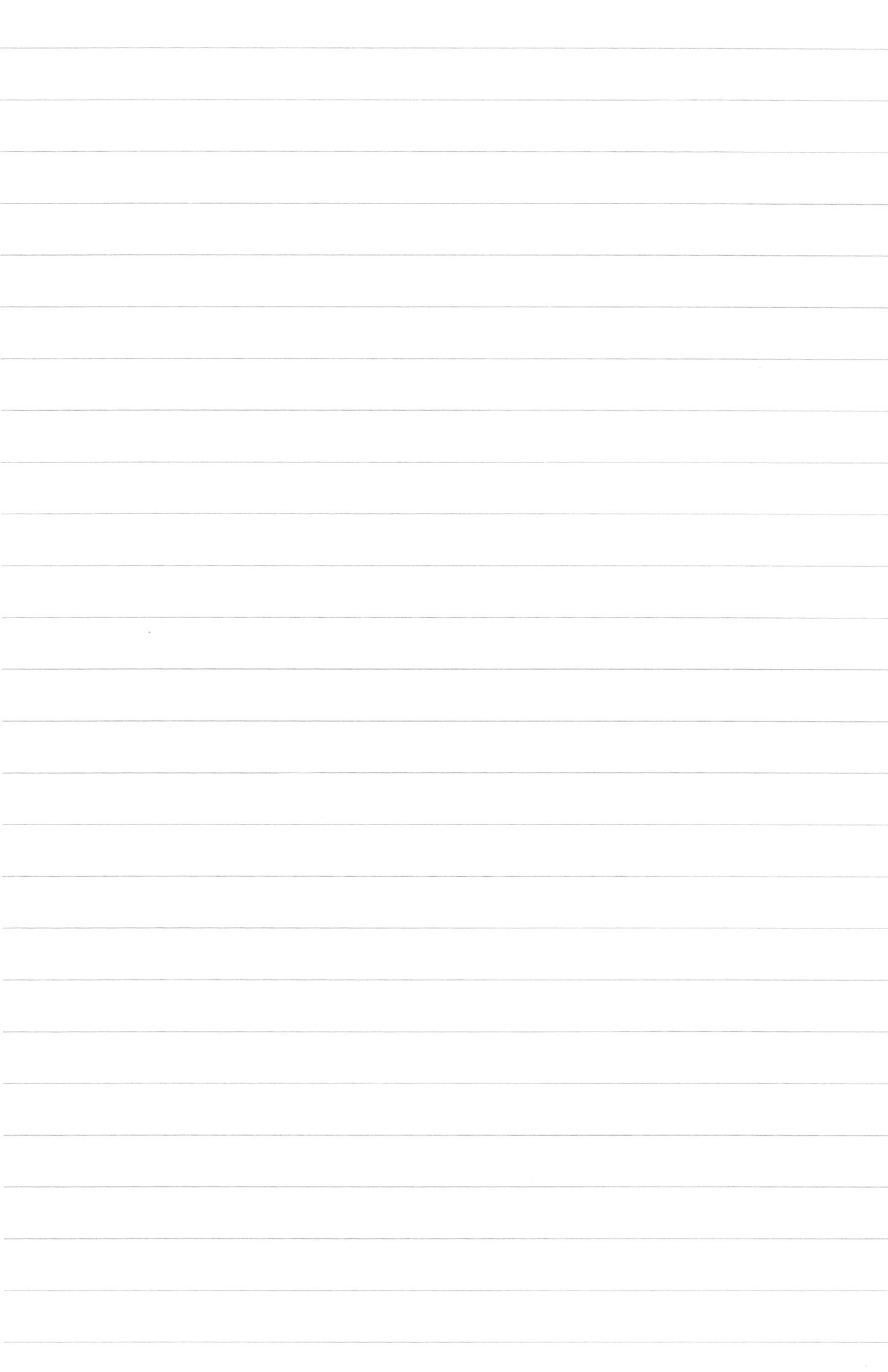

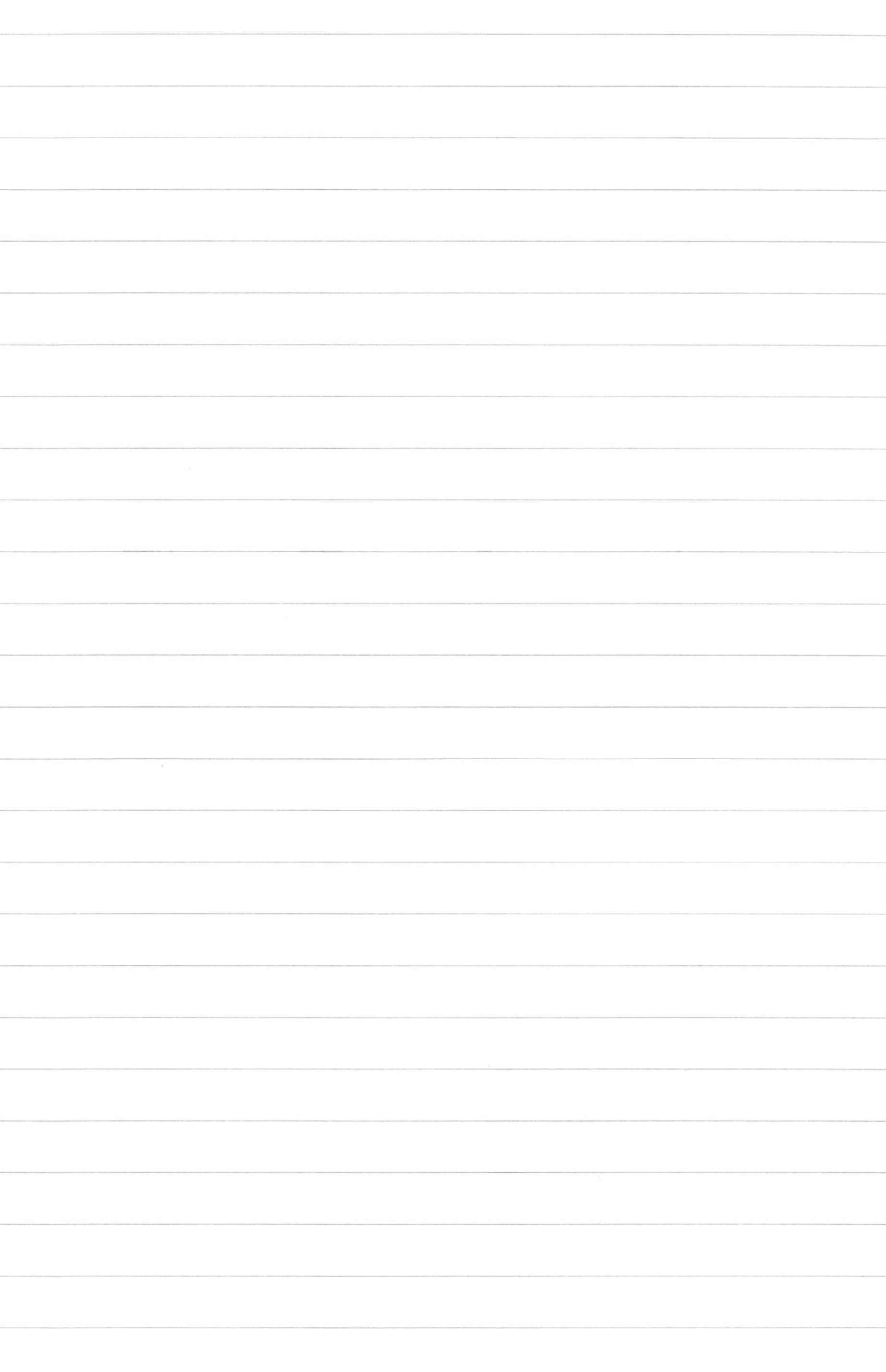

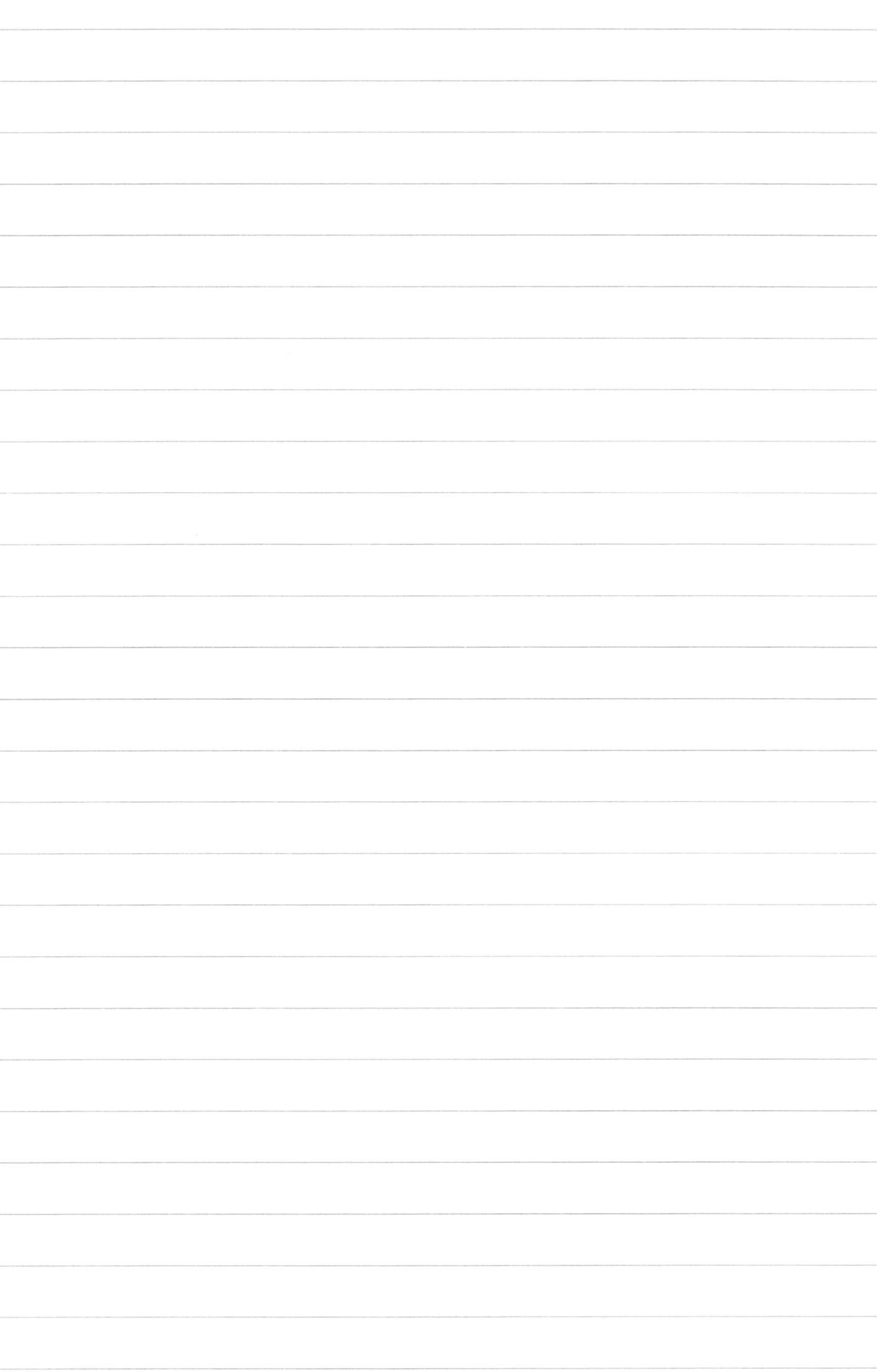

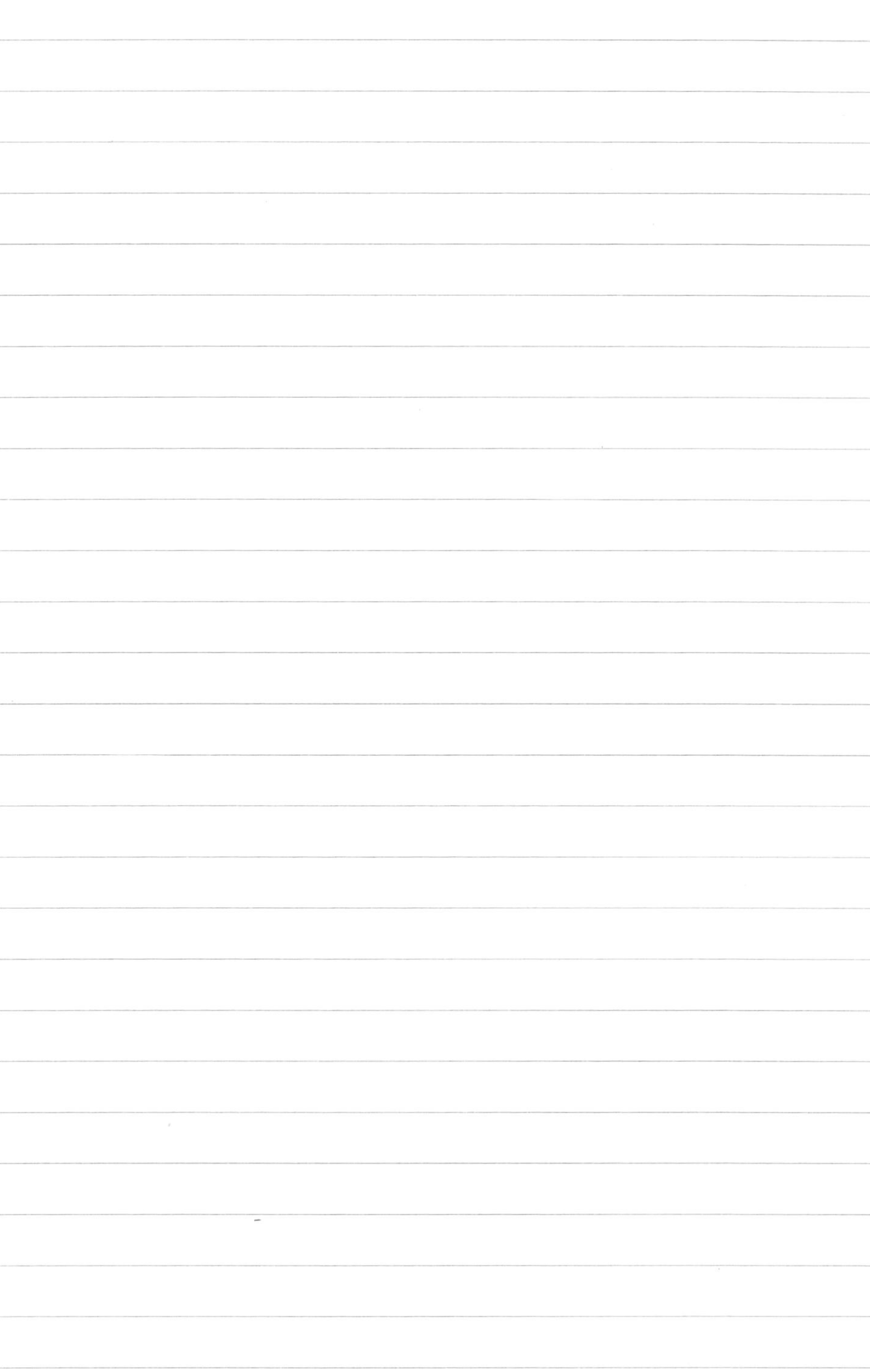

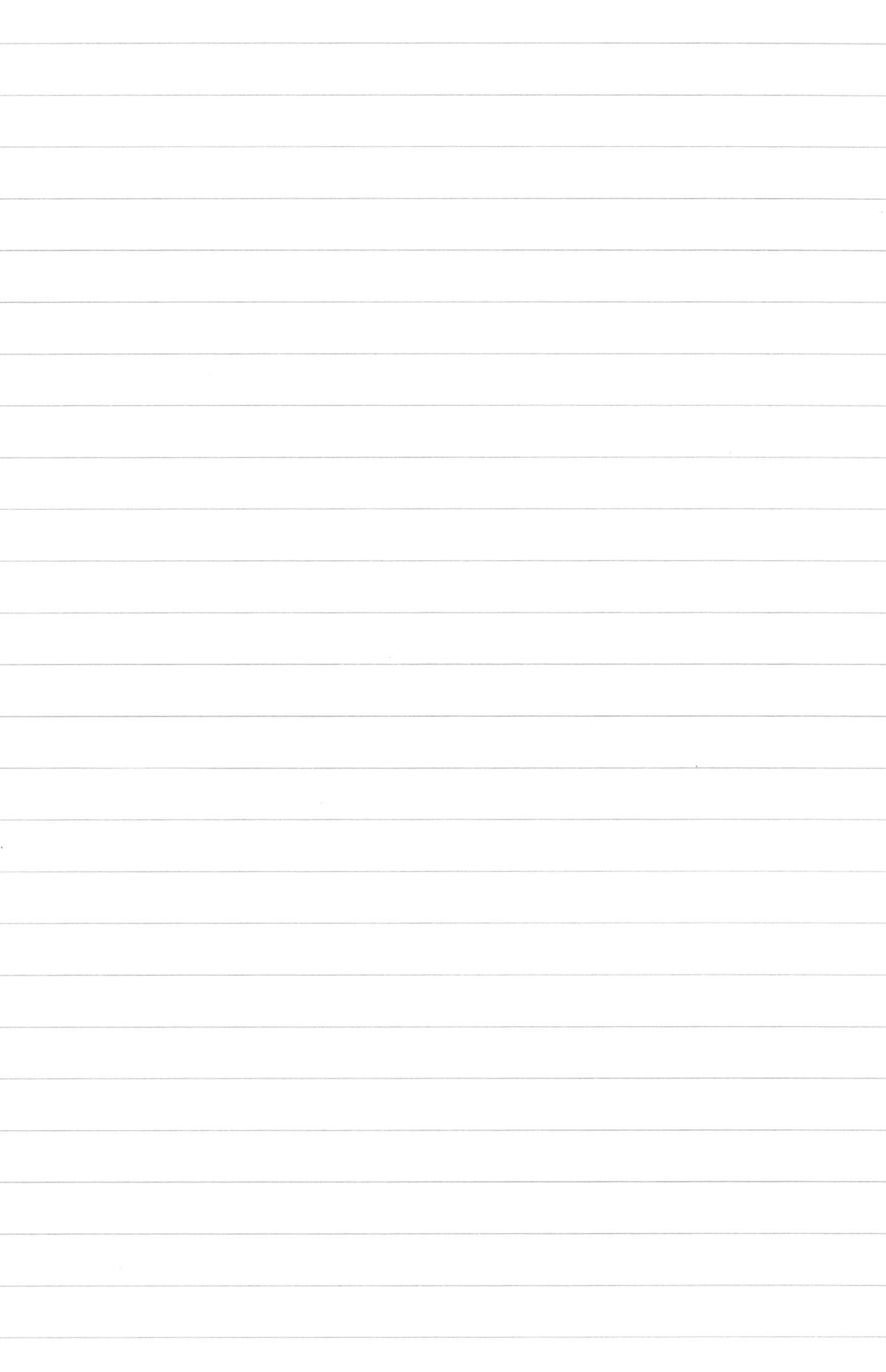

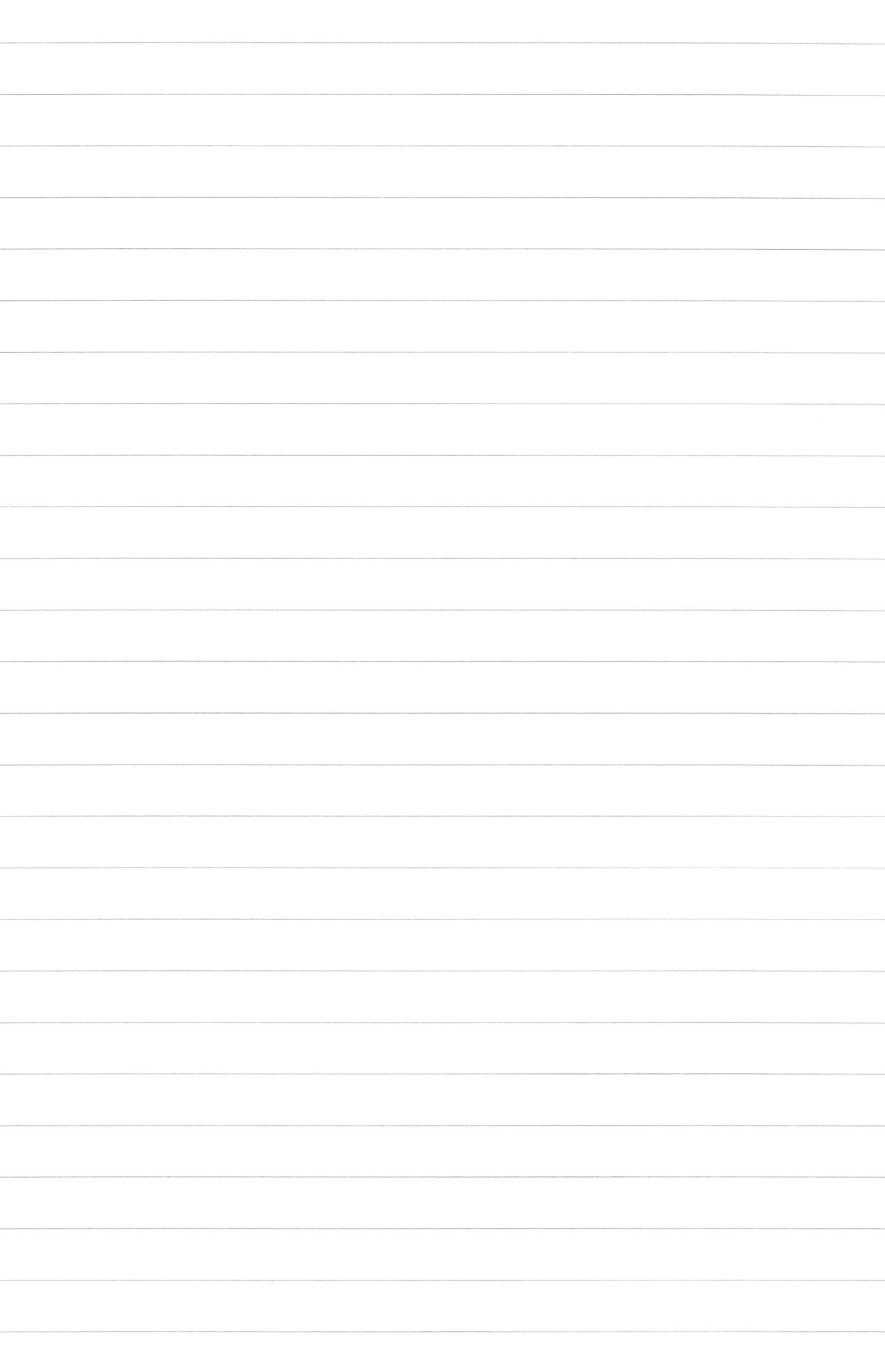

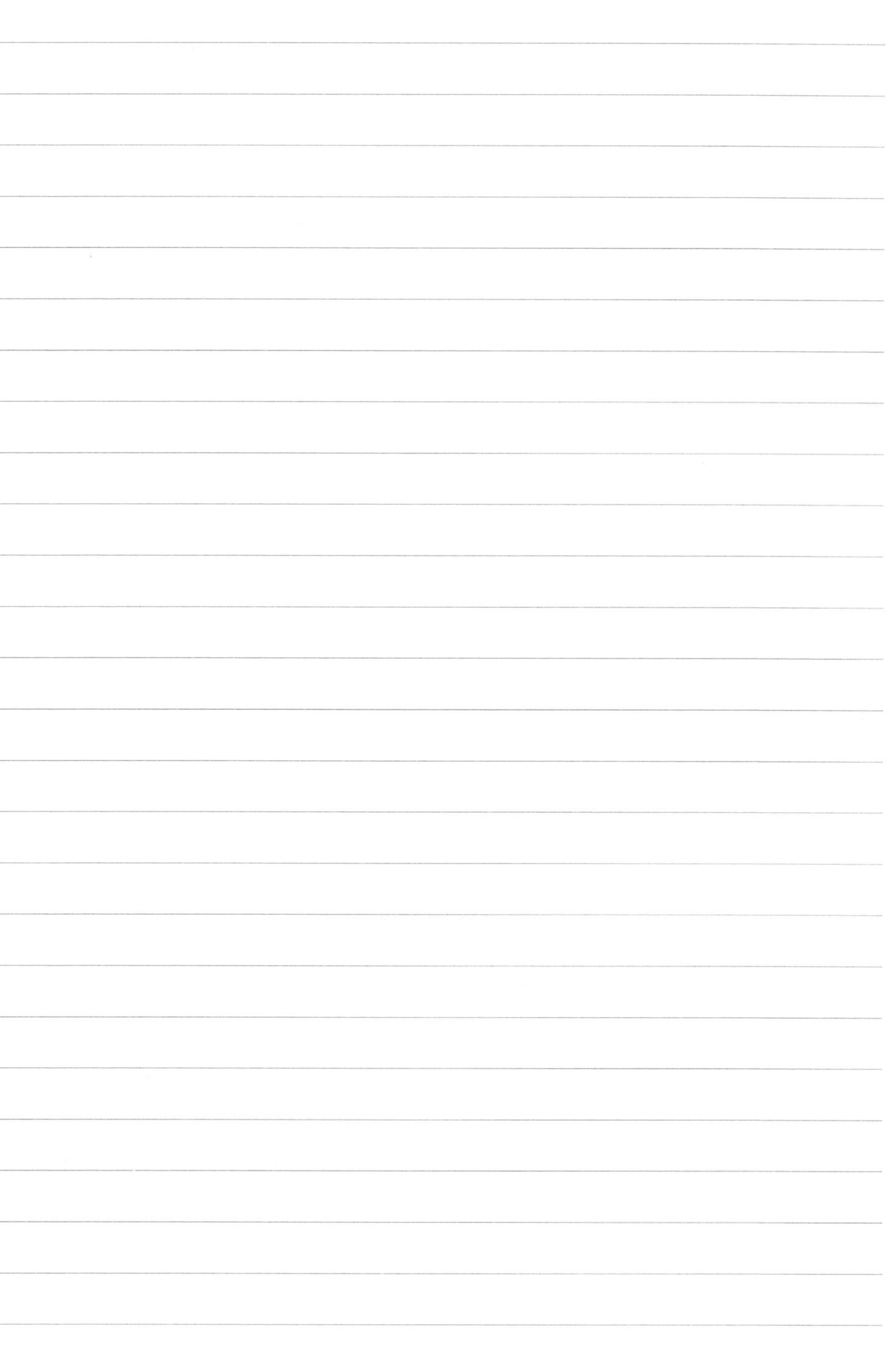

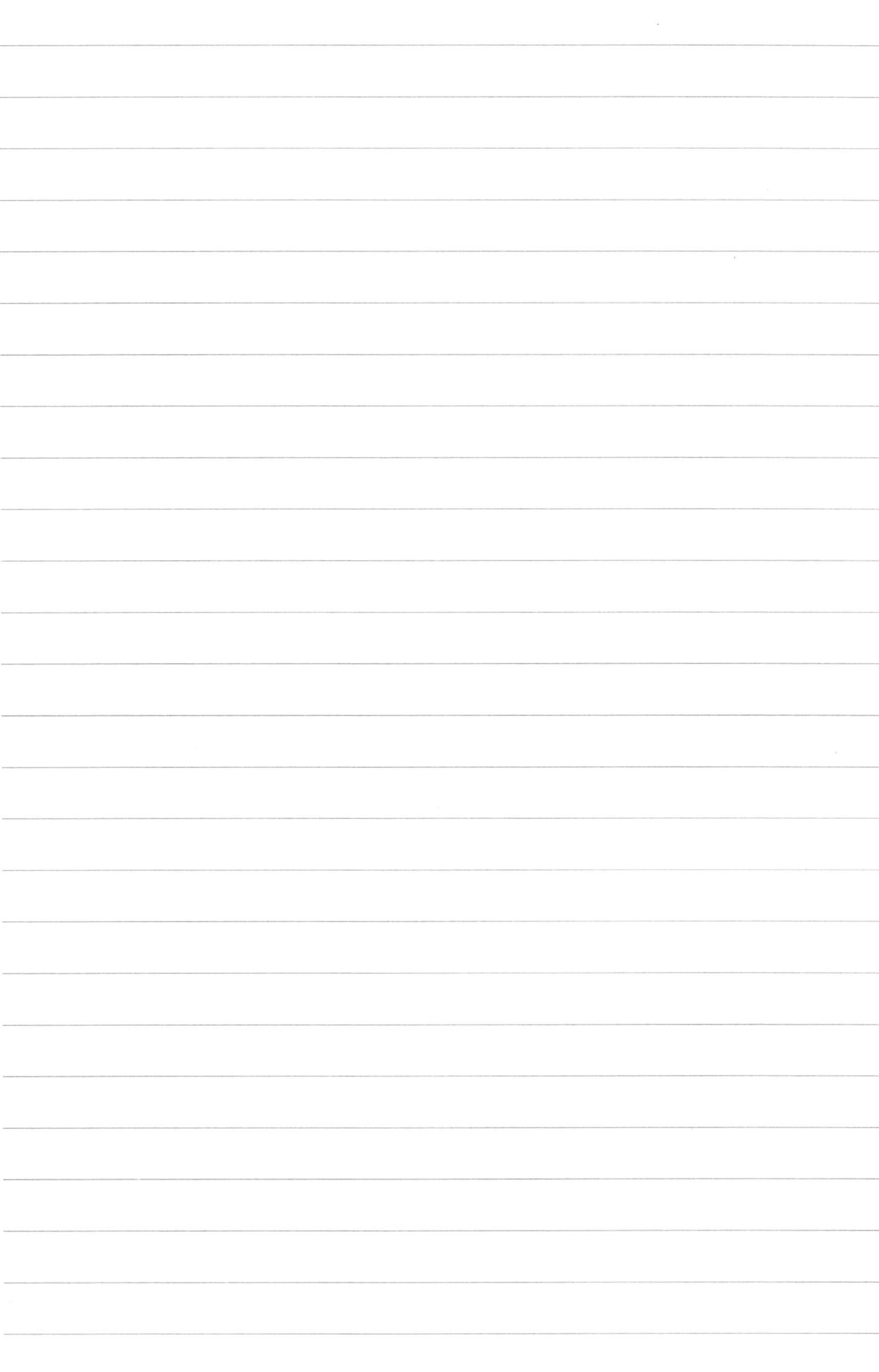

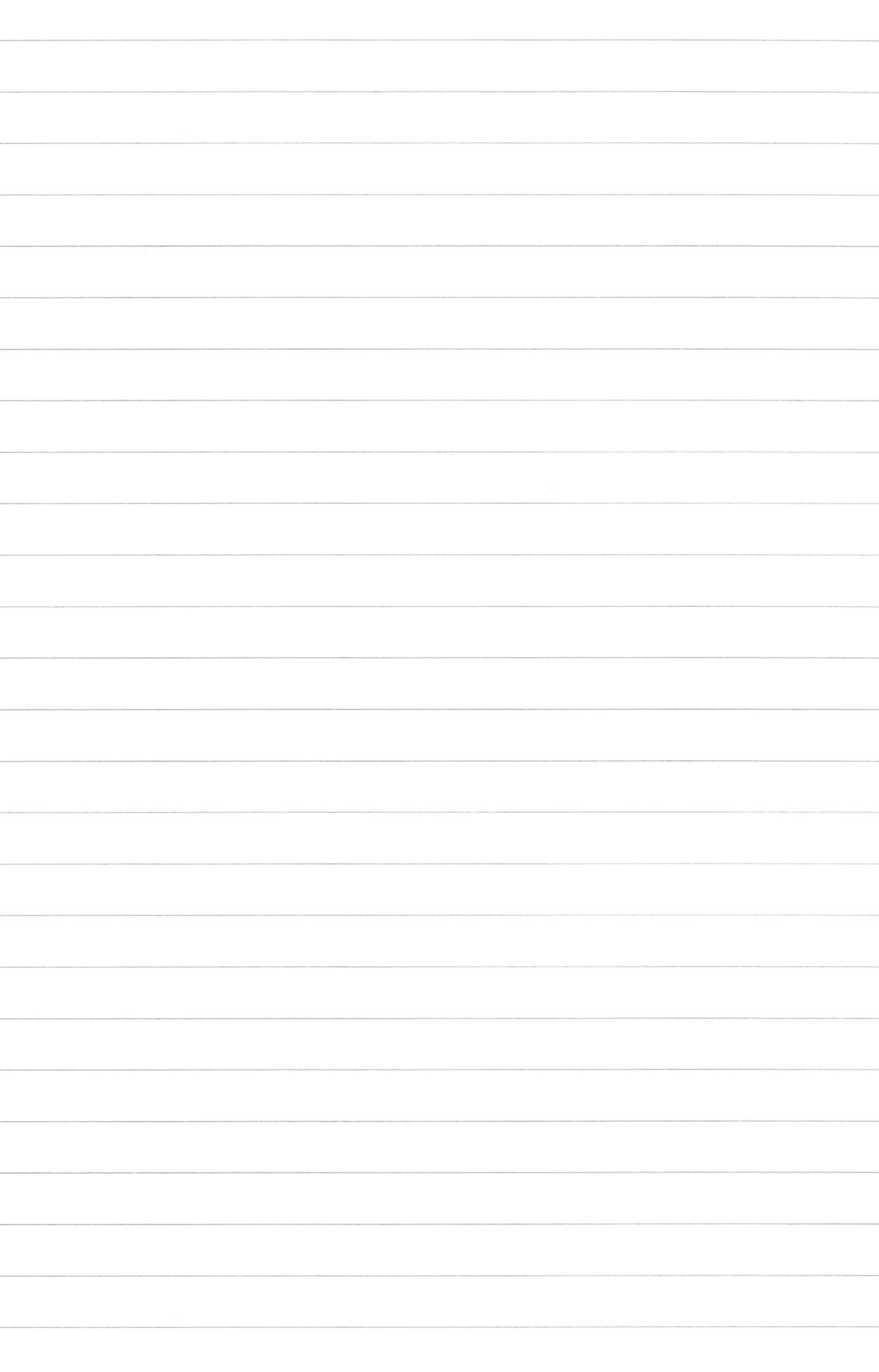

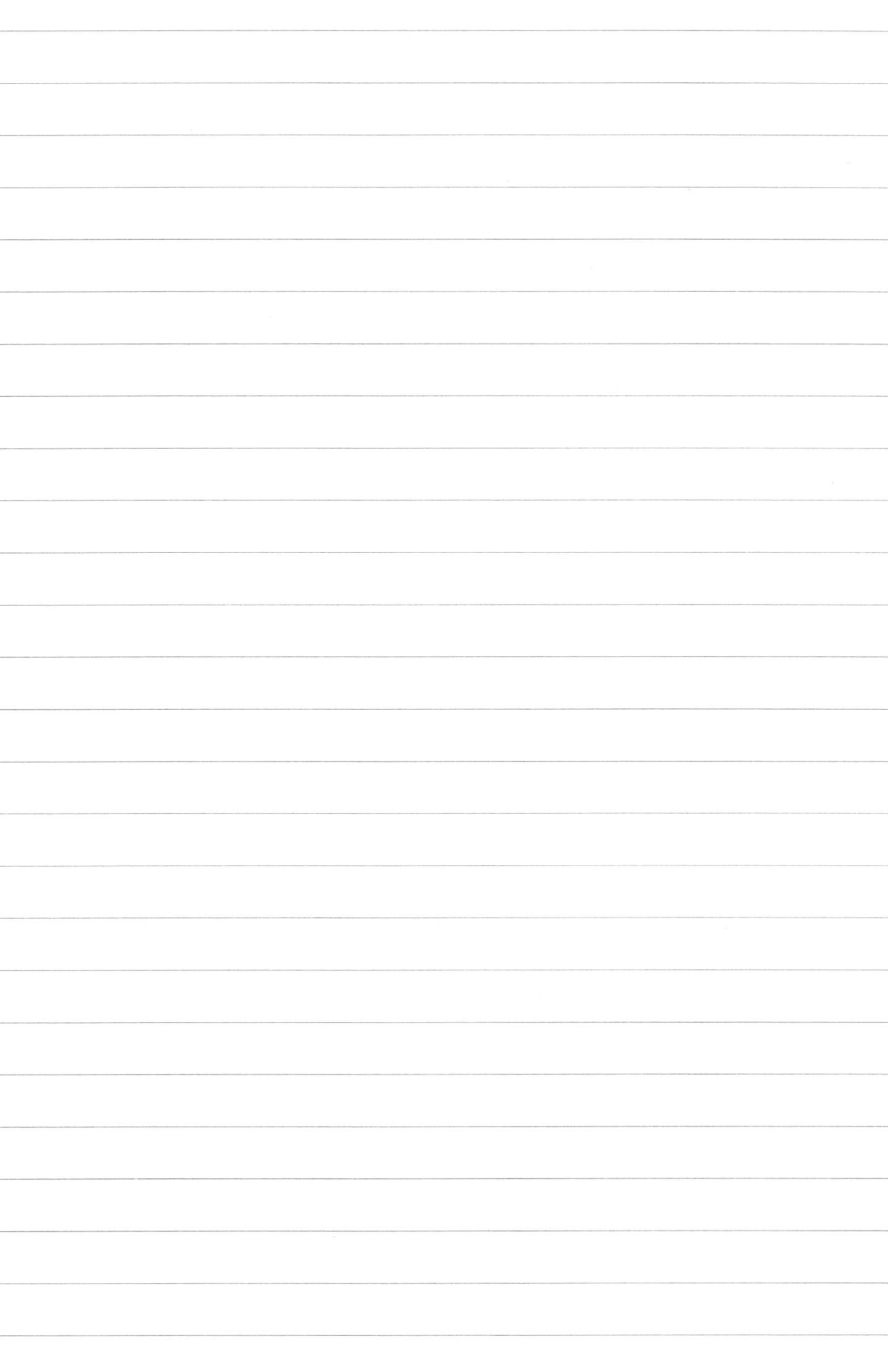

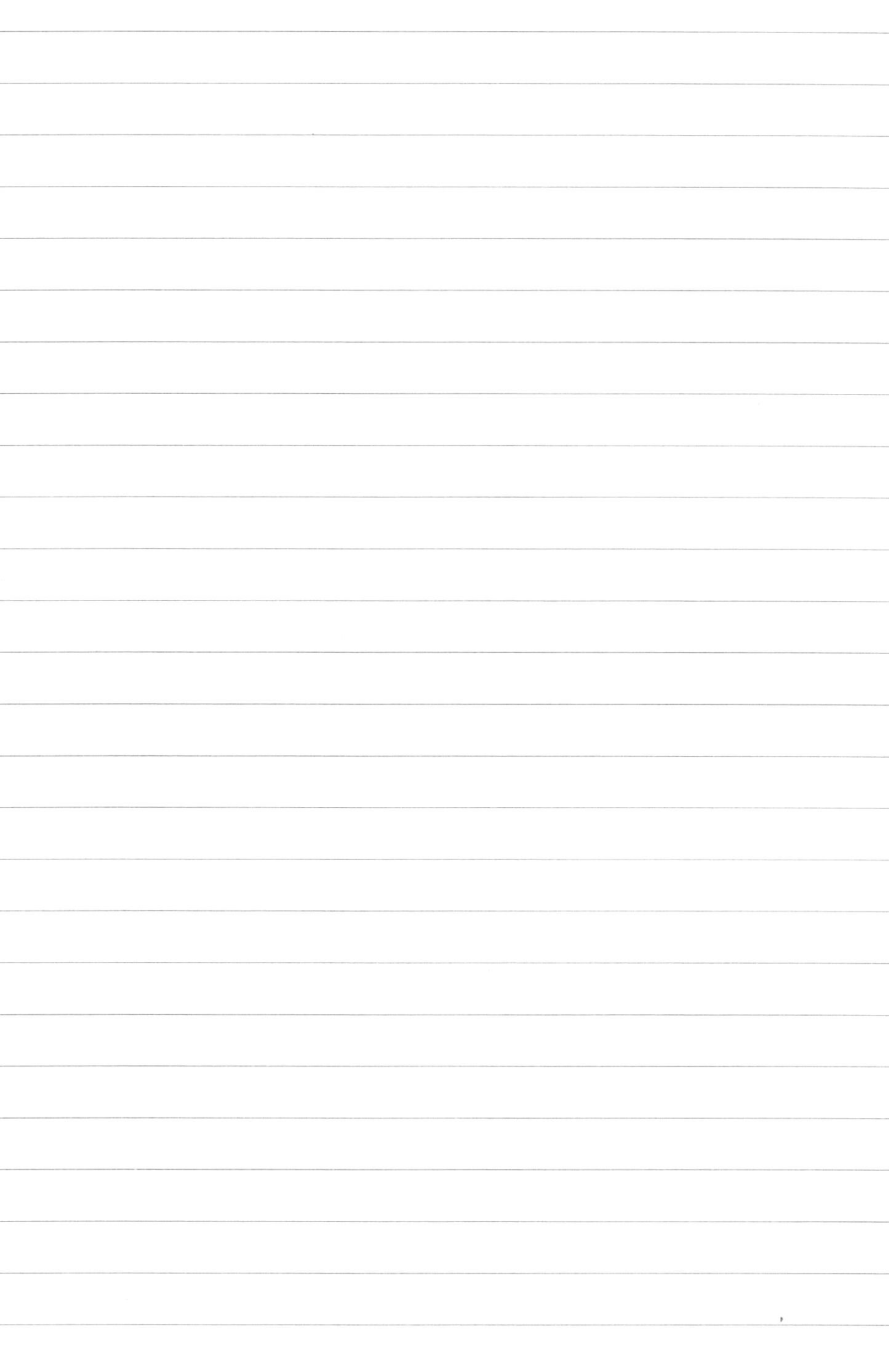

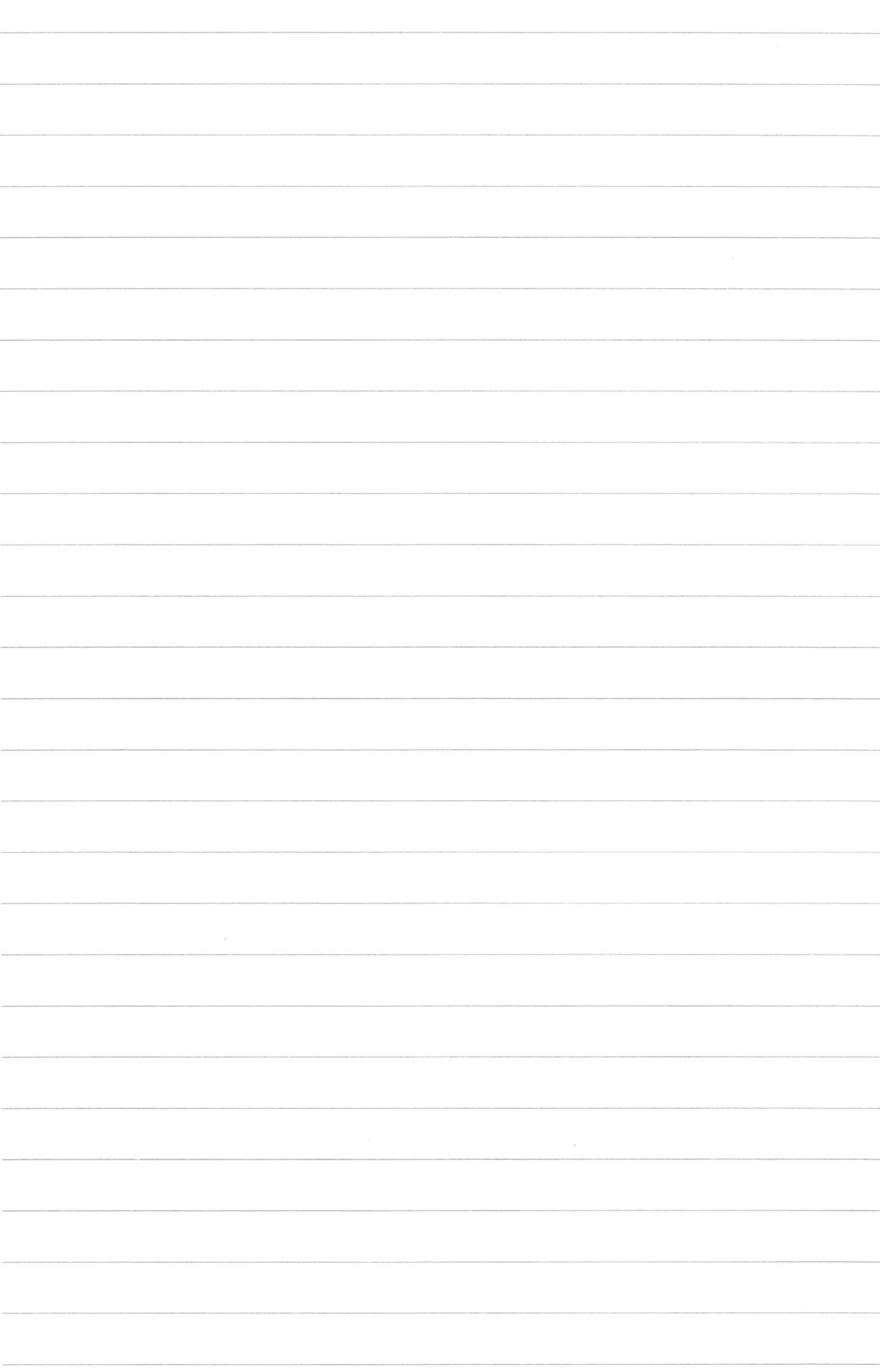

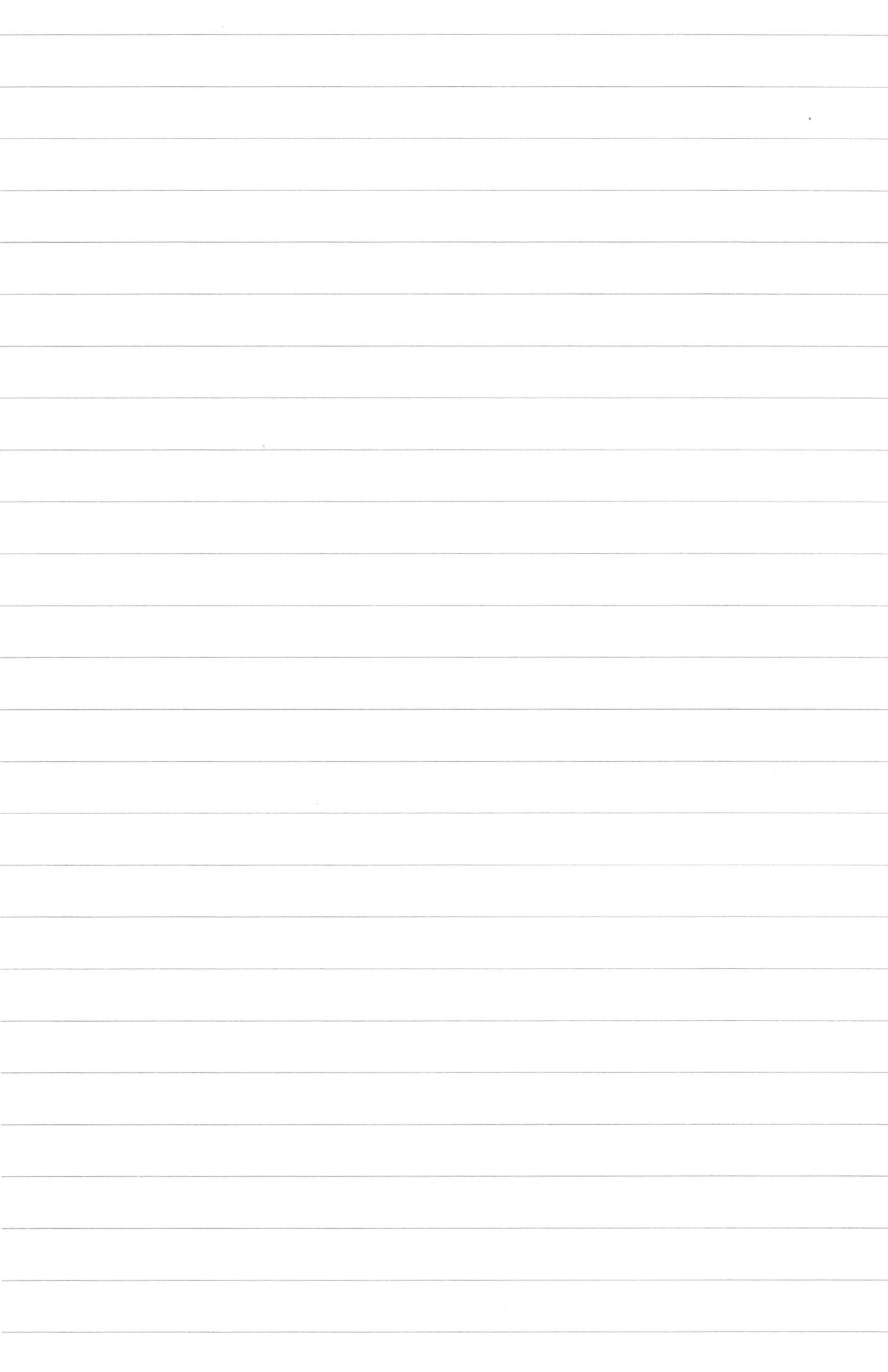

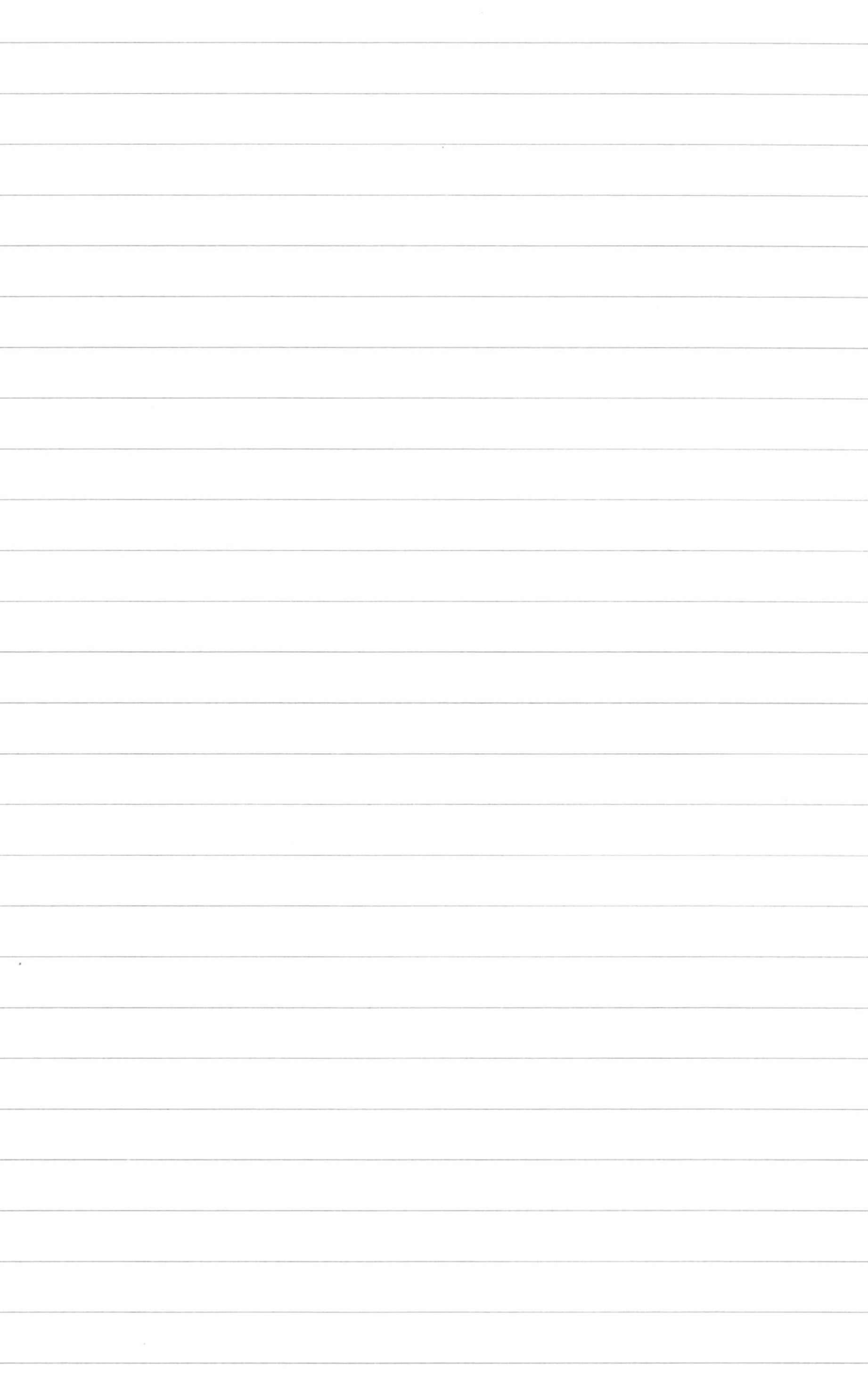

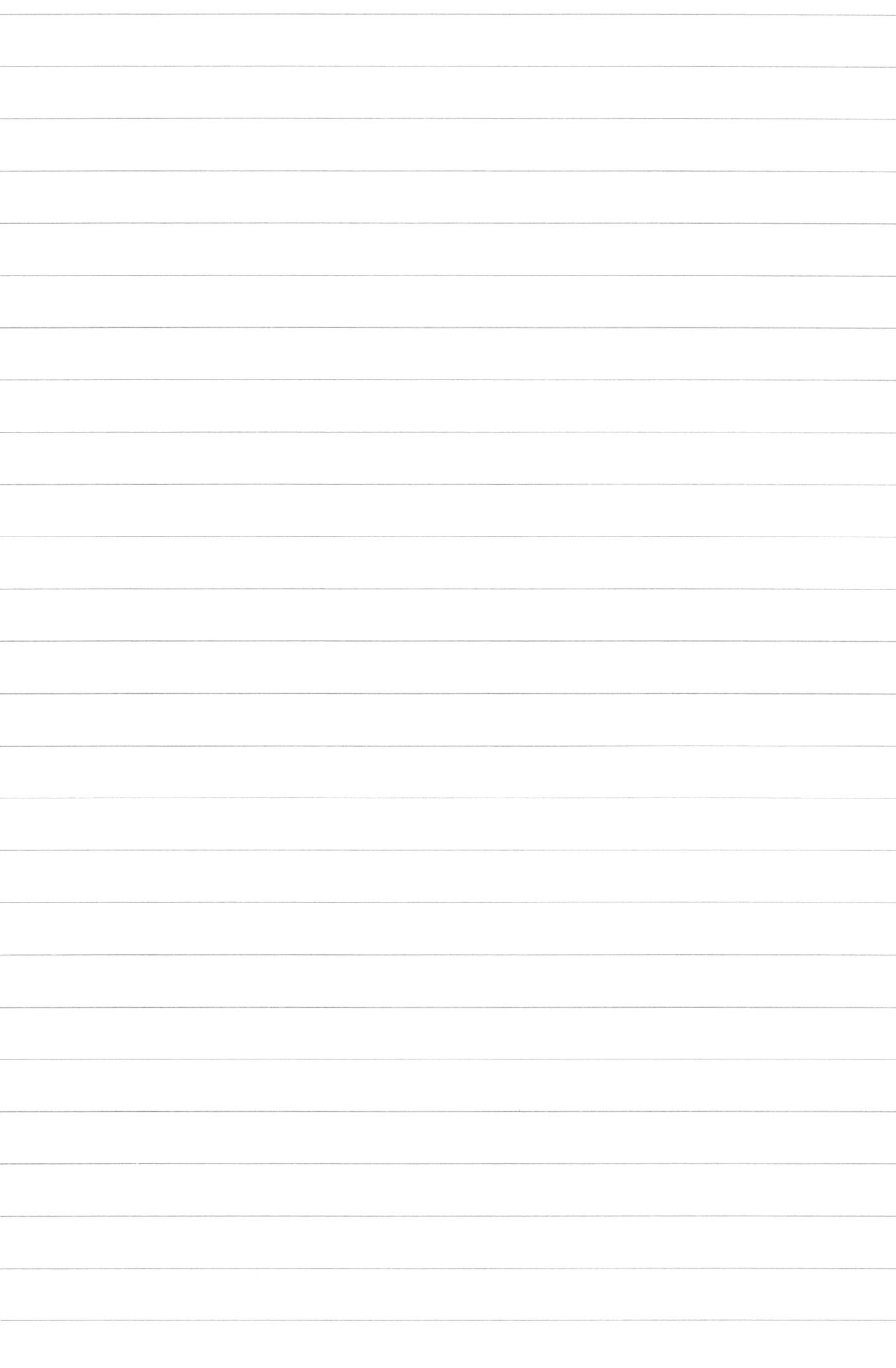

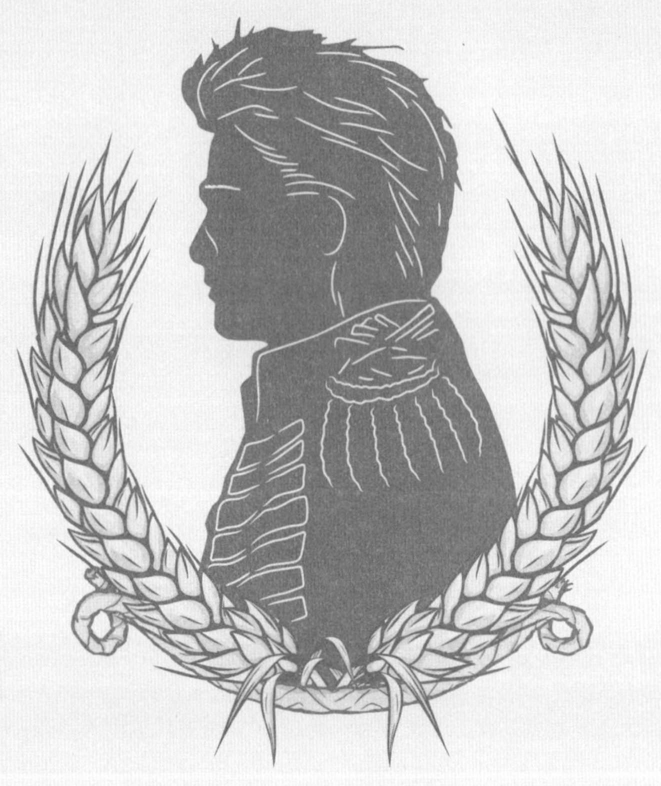

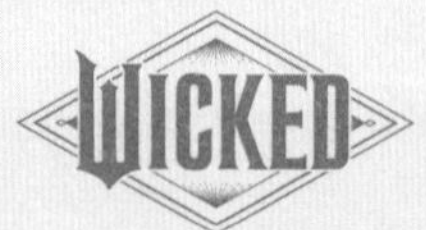

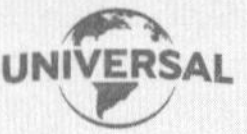

INSIGHTS
insighteditions.com

MANUFACTURED IN VIETNAM

10 9 8 7 6 5 4 3 2 1

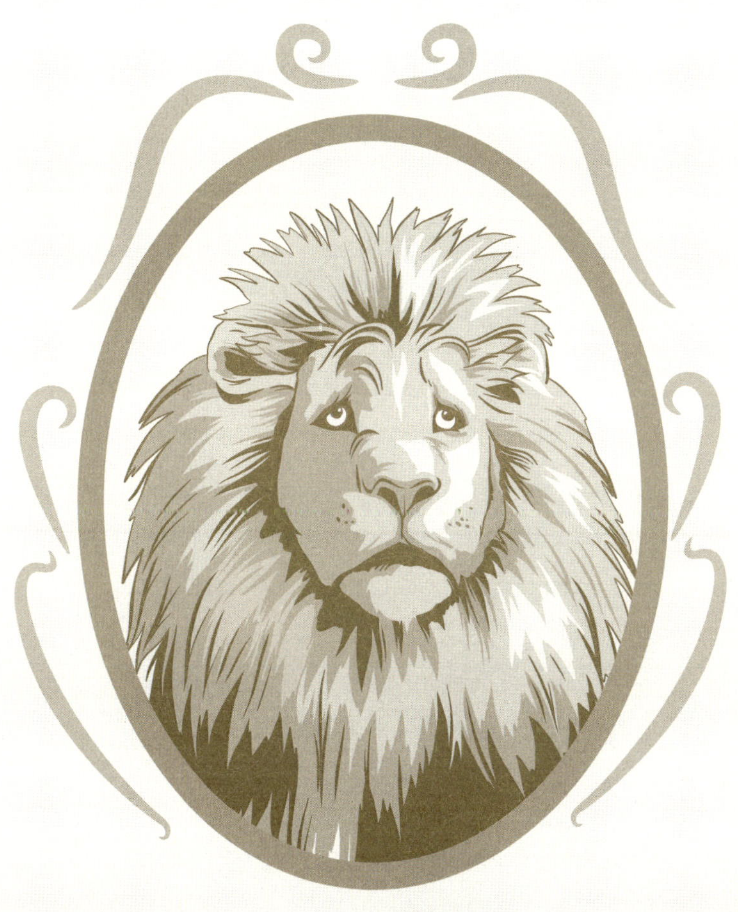

PROPERTY OF

____

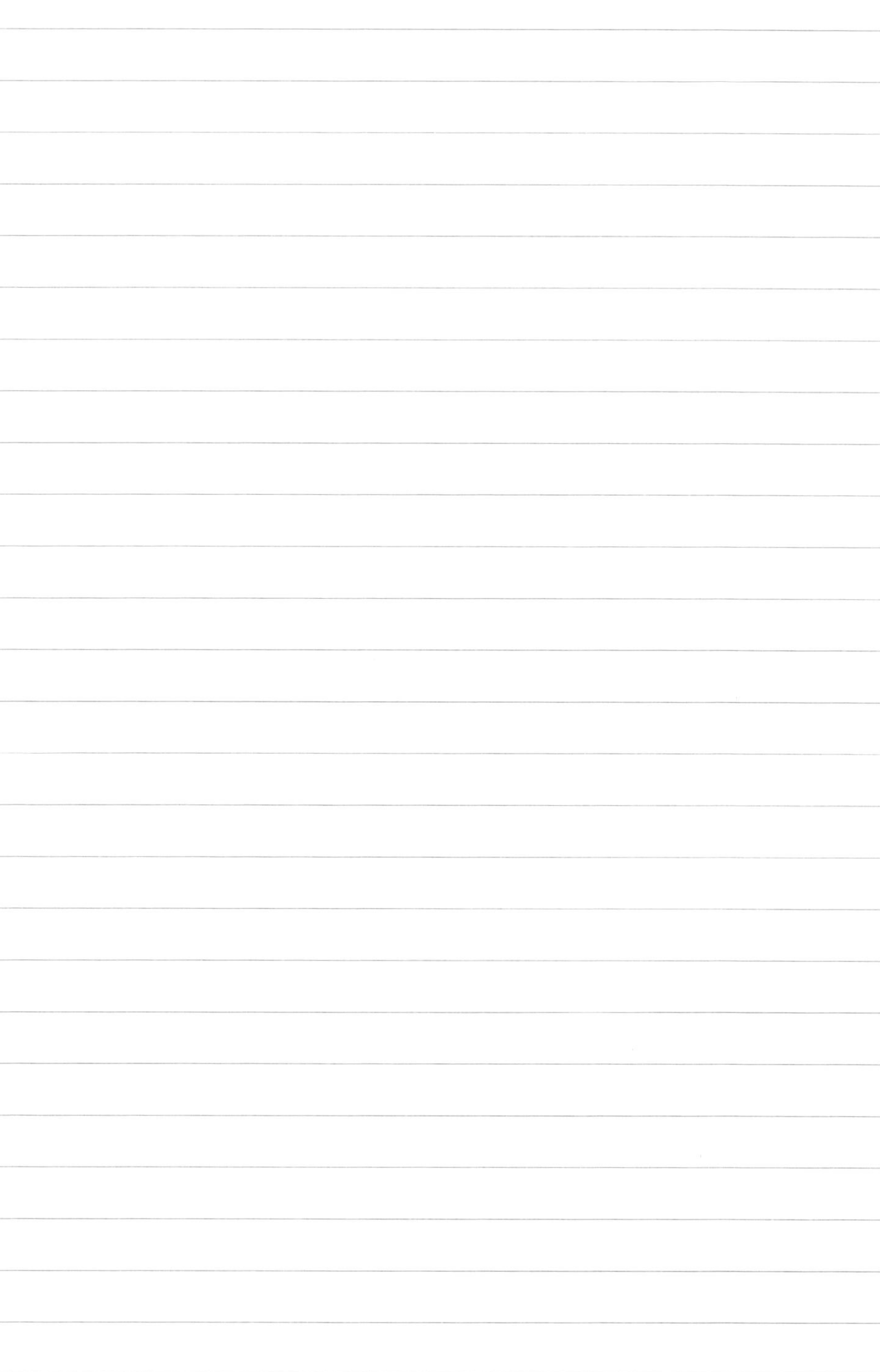

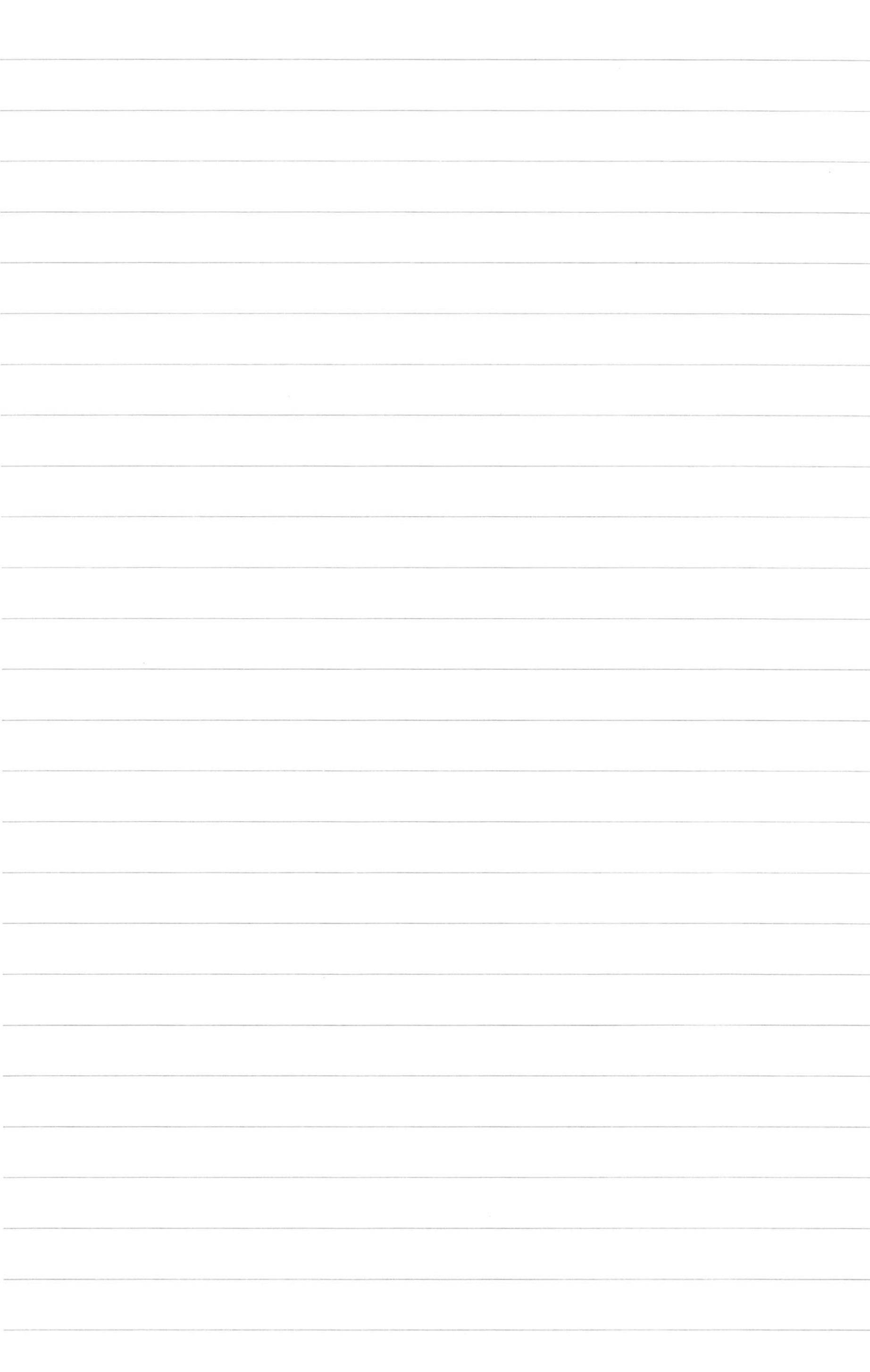

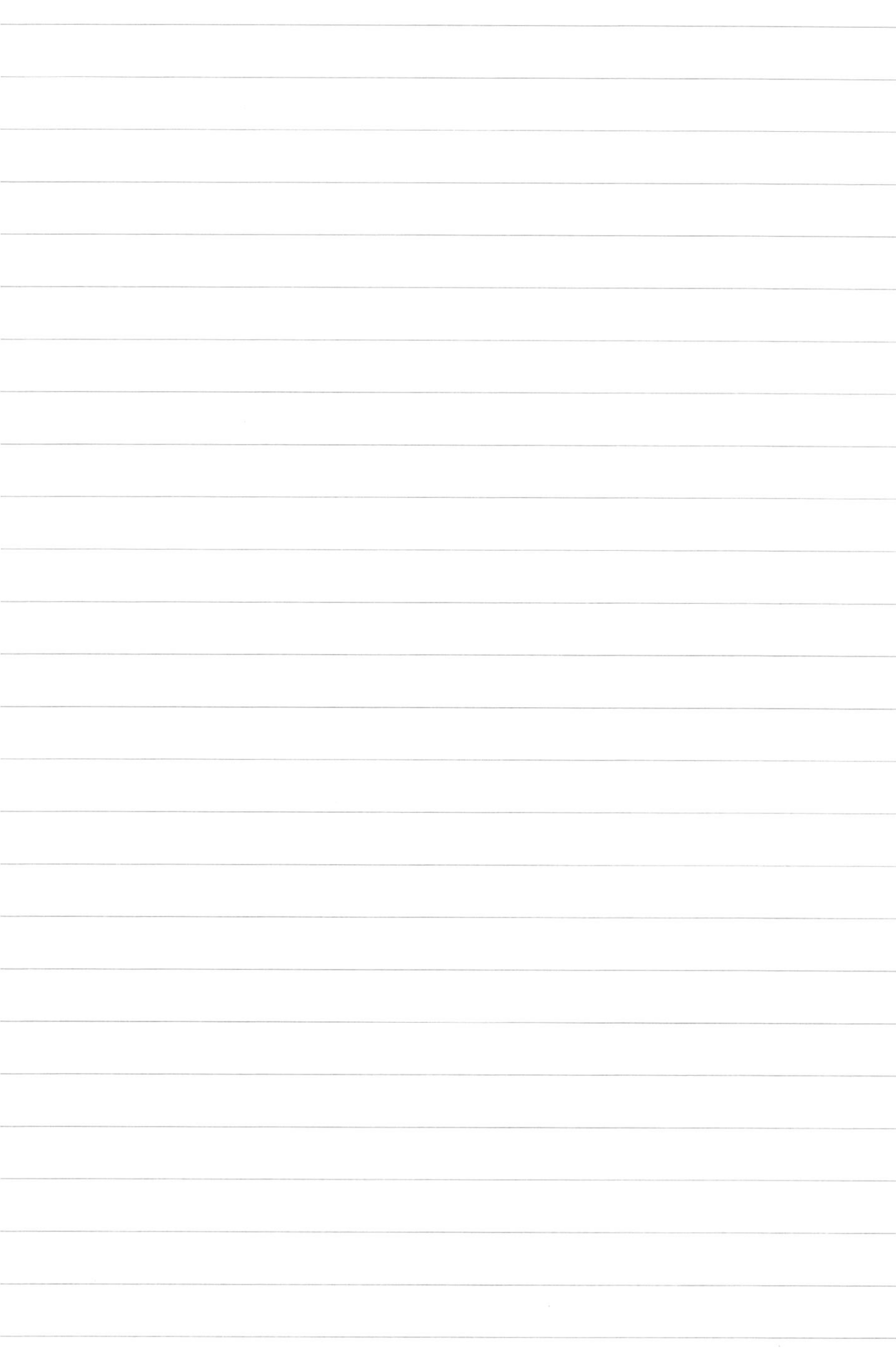

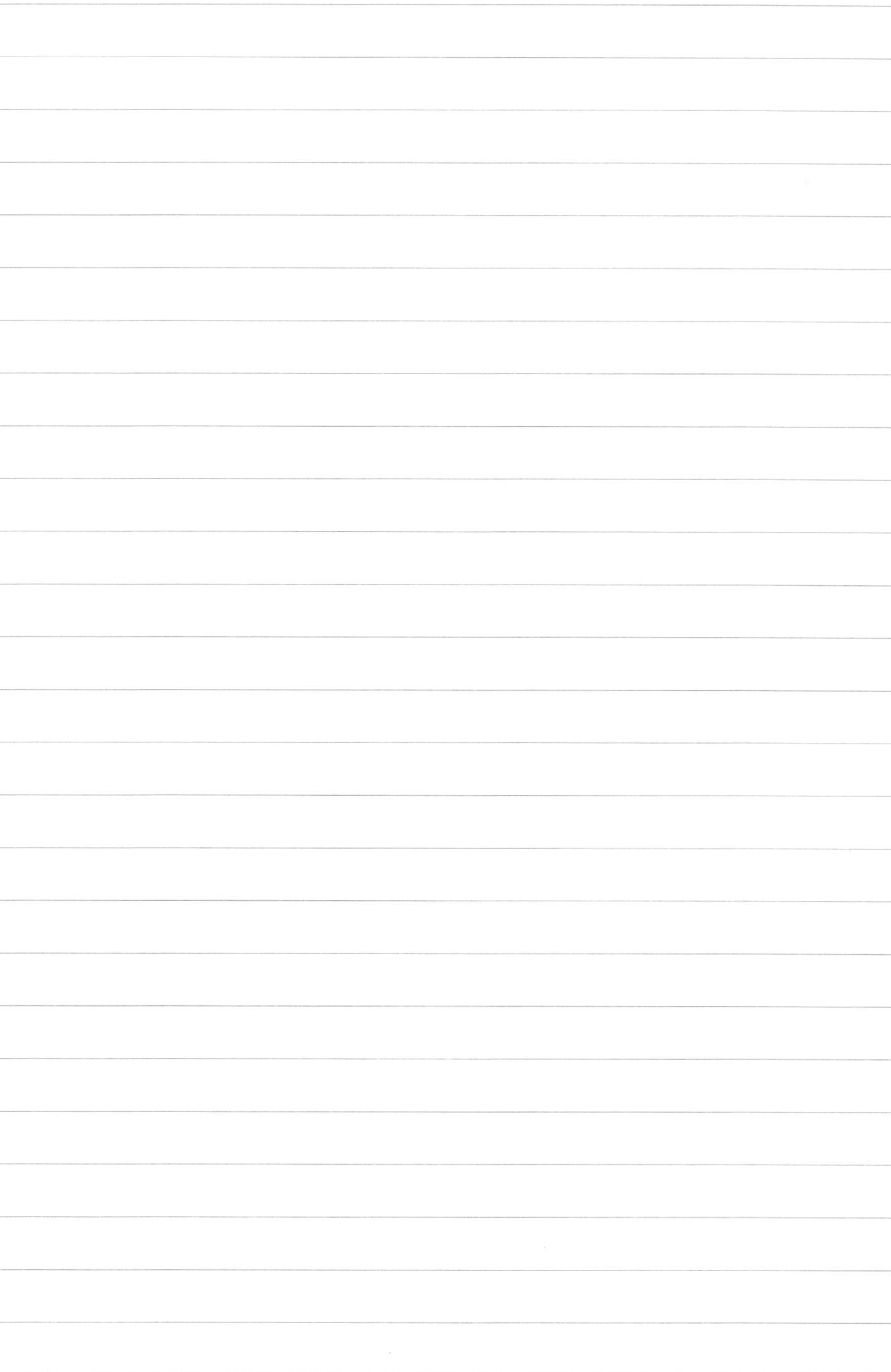

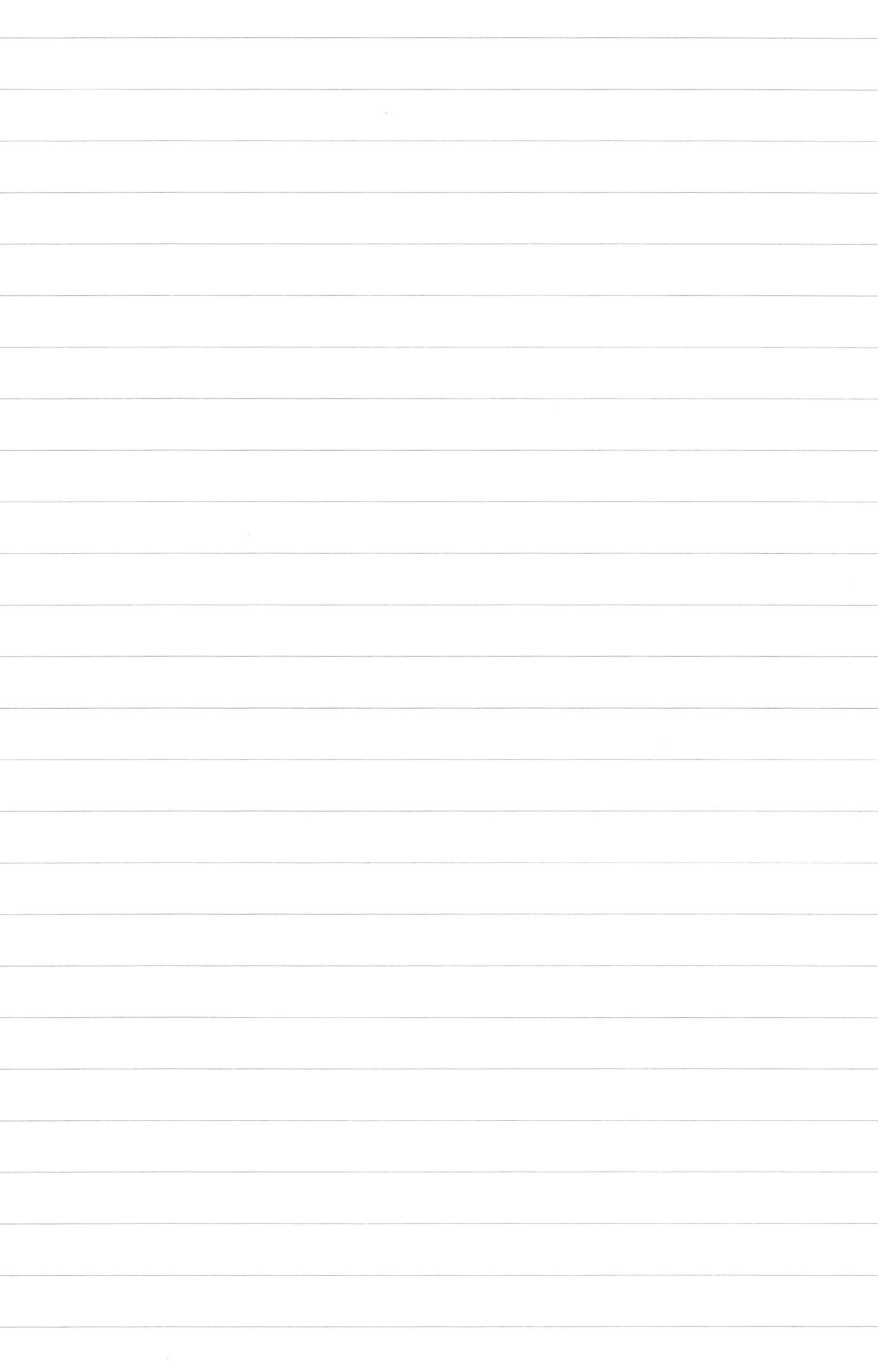

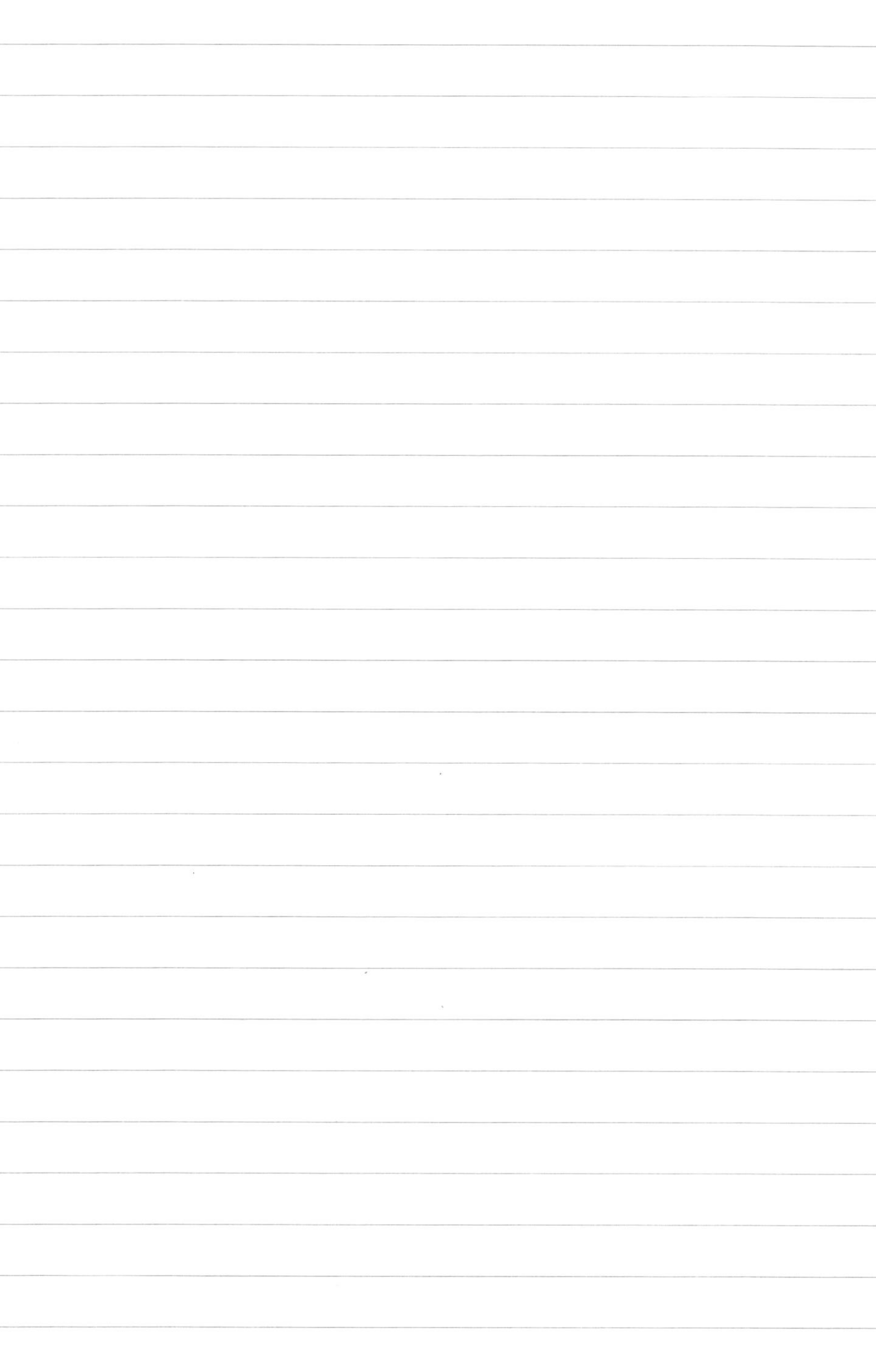

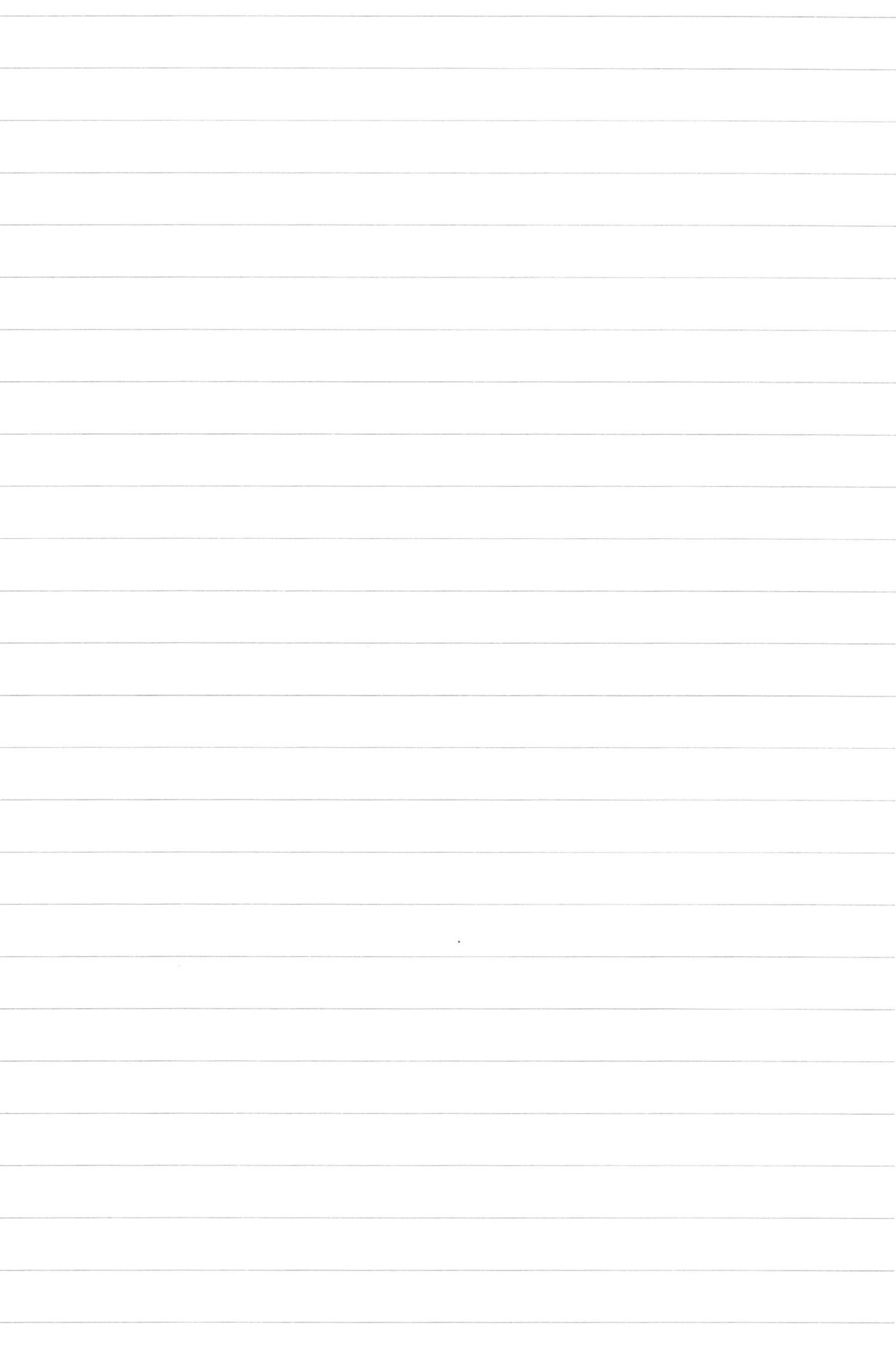

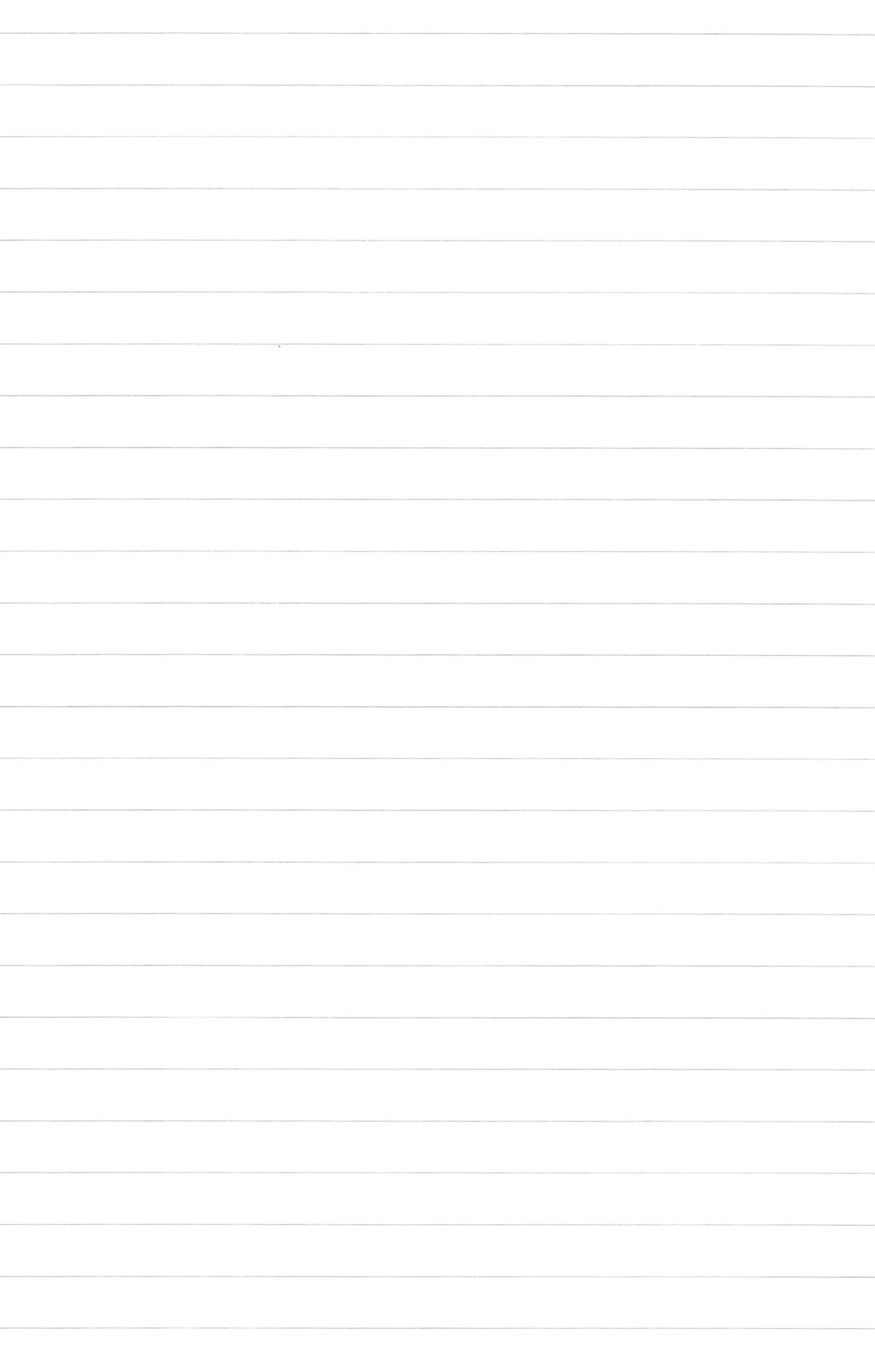

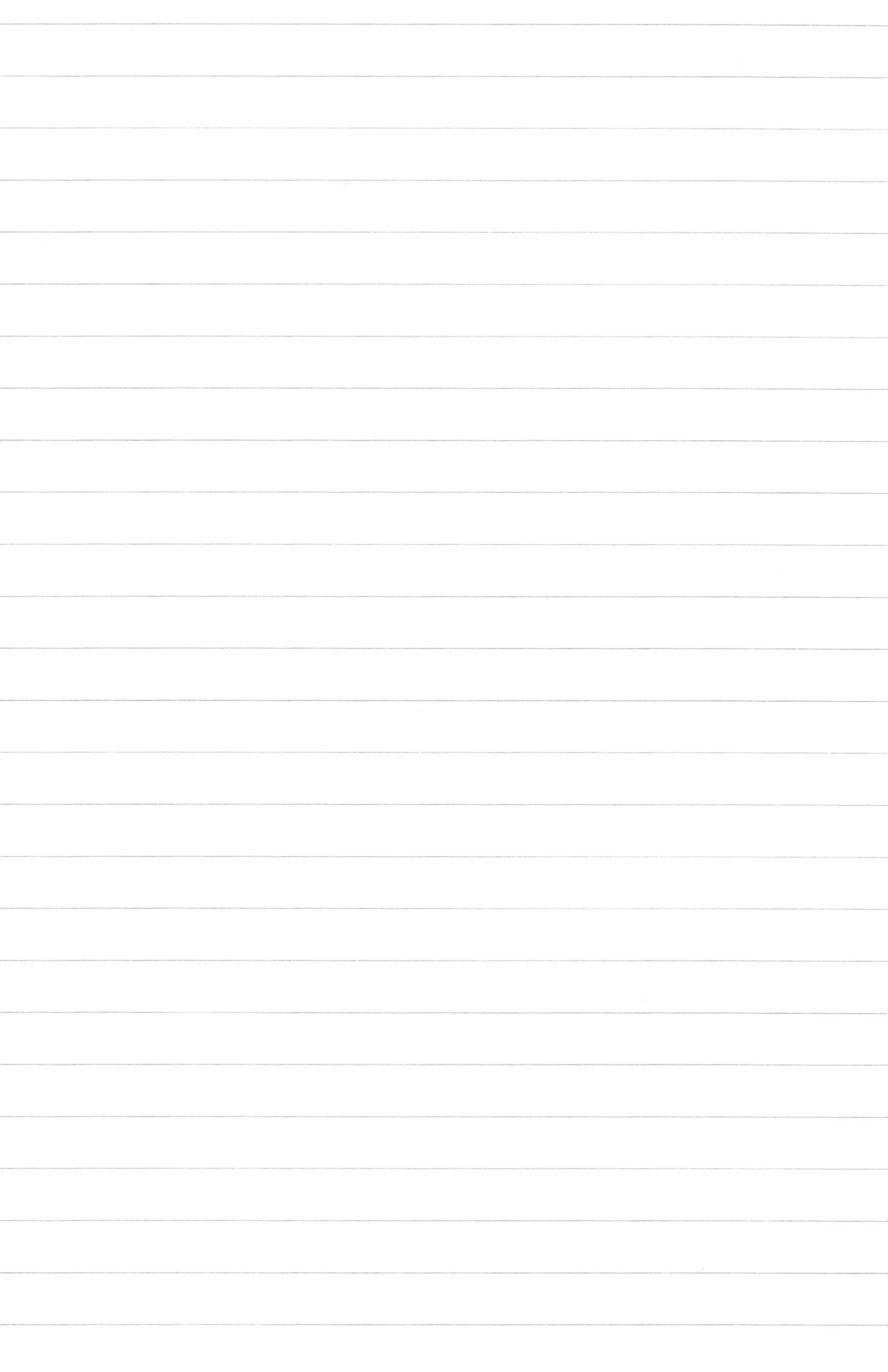

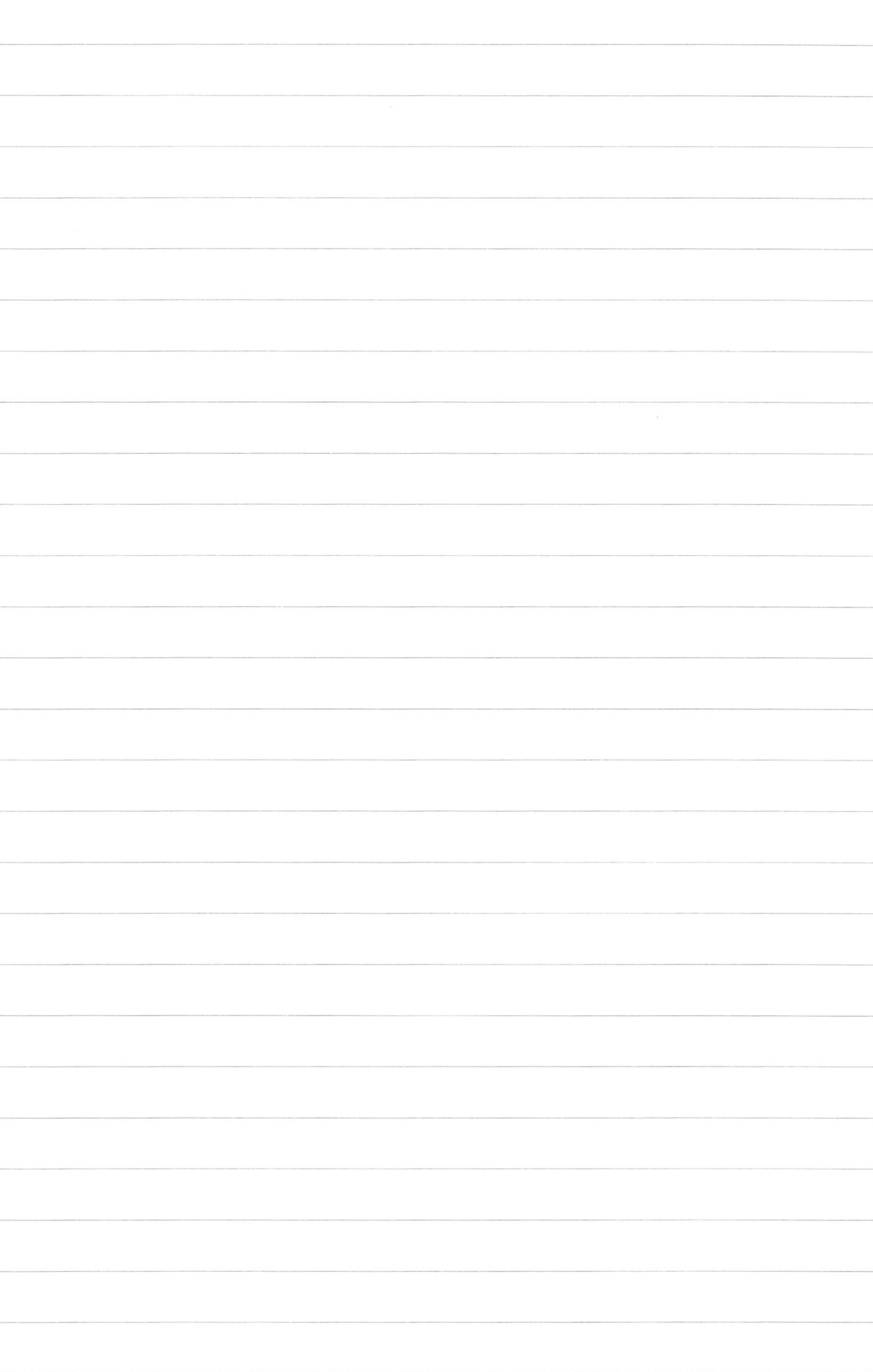

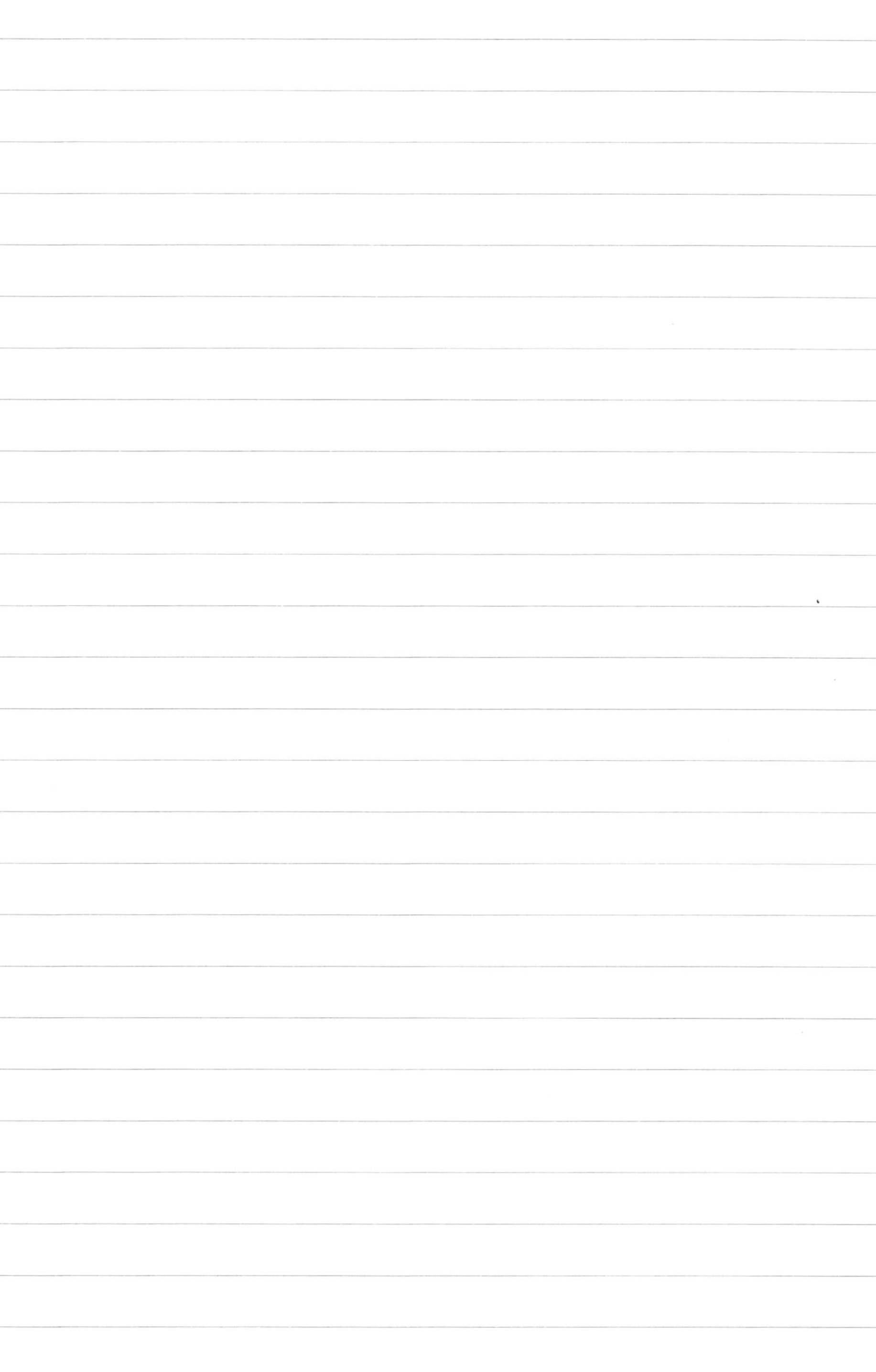

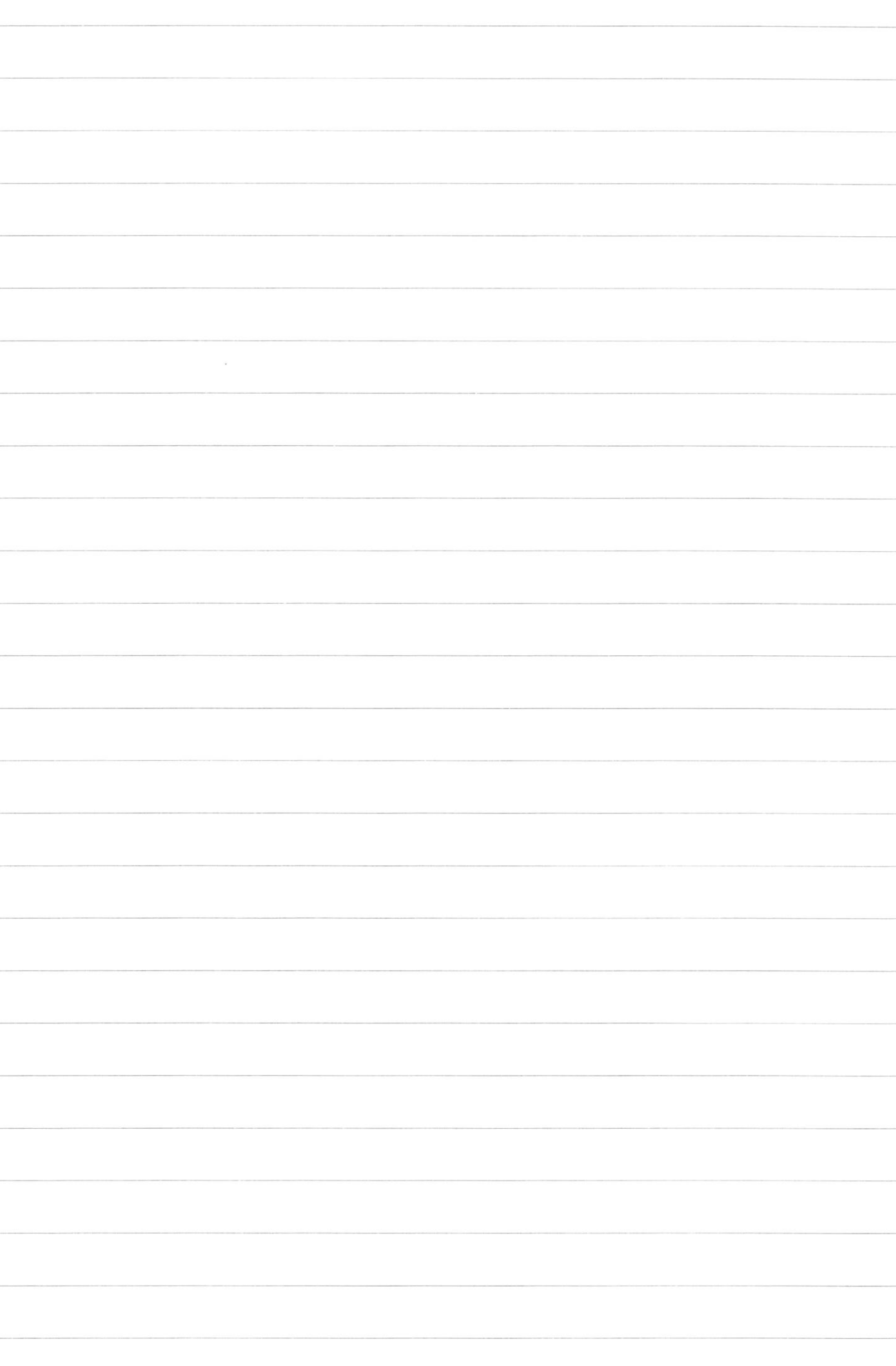

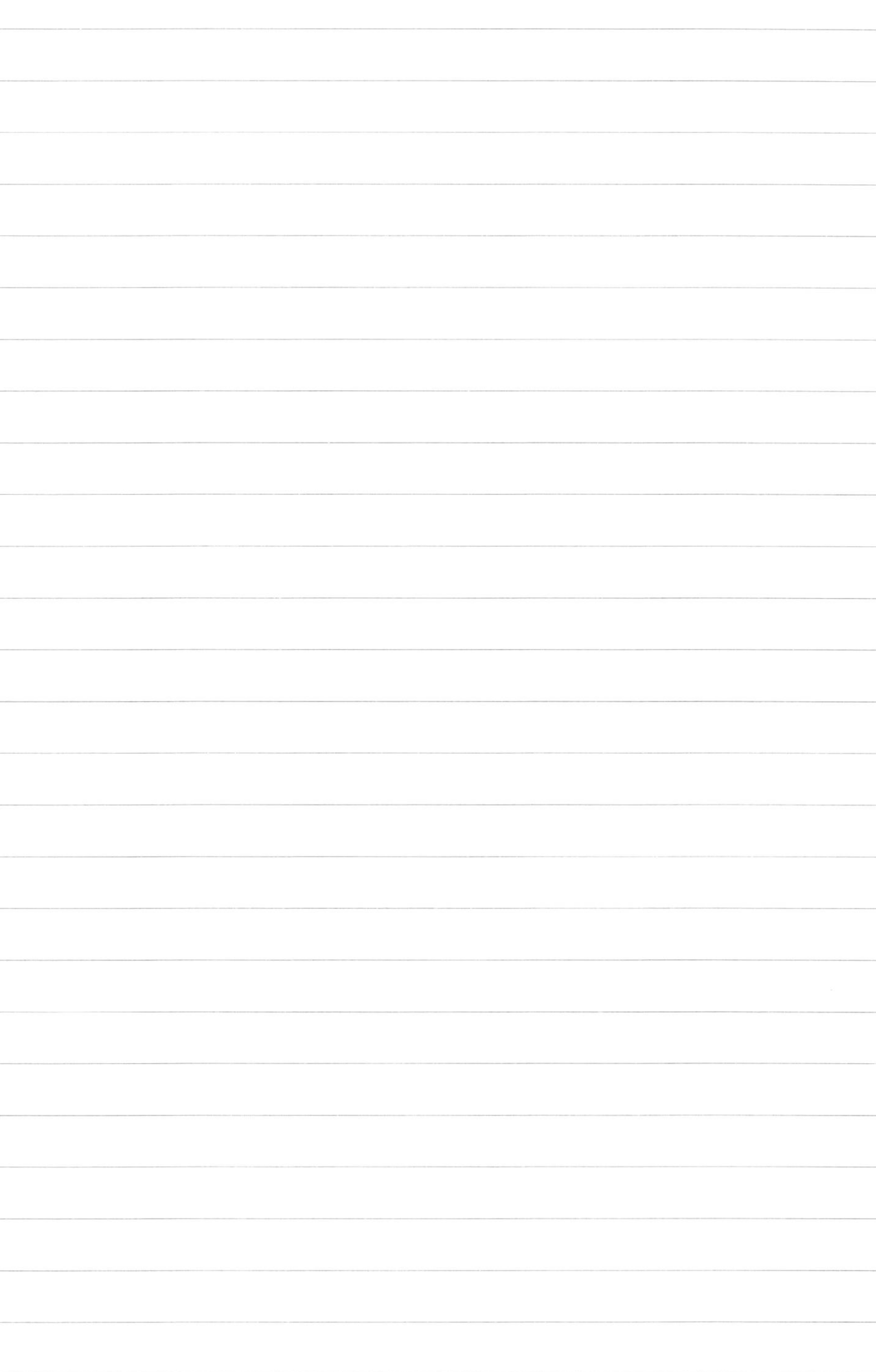

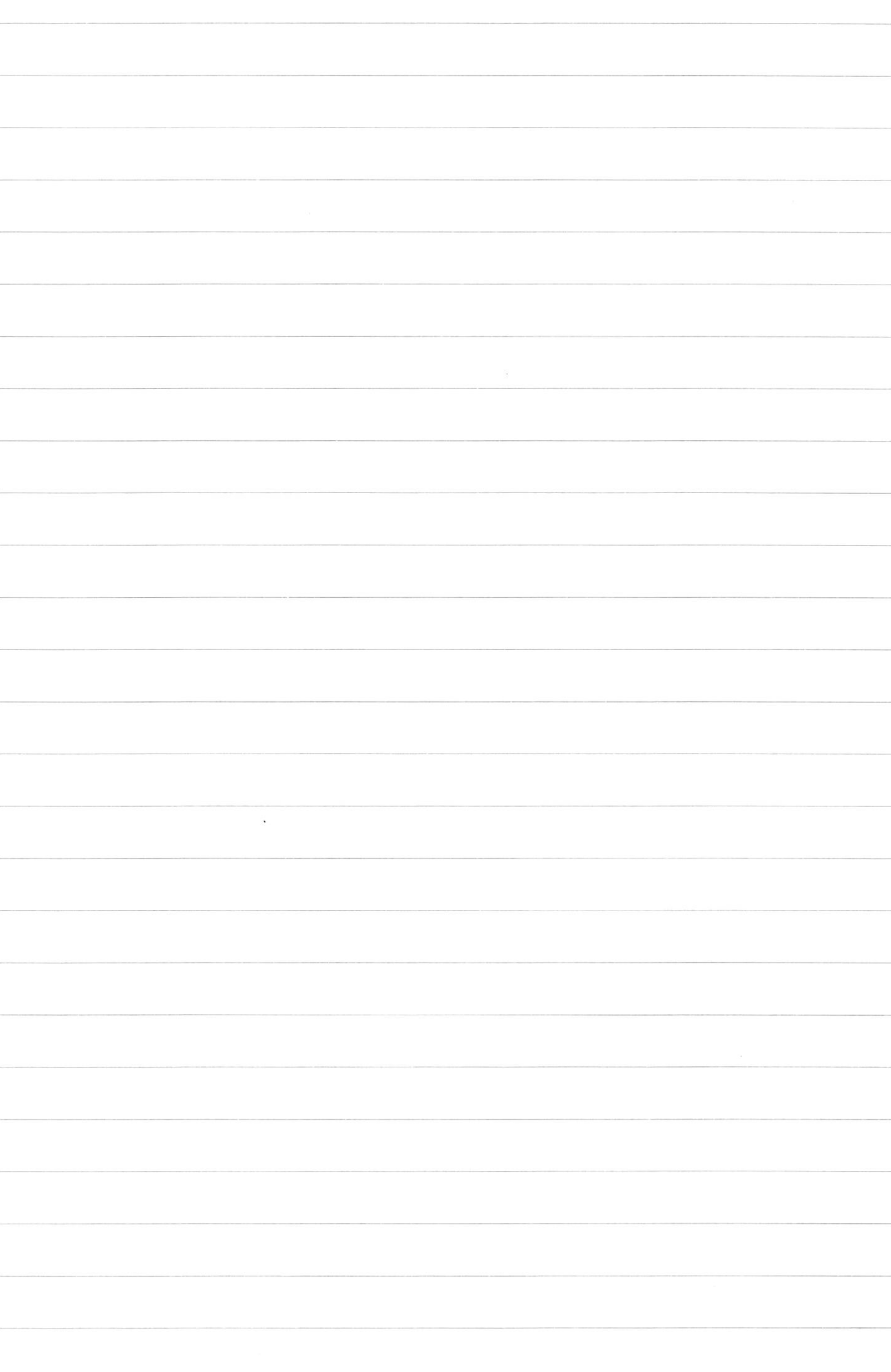

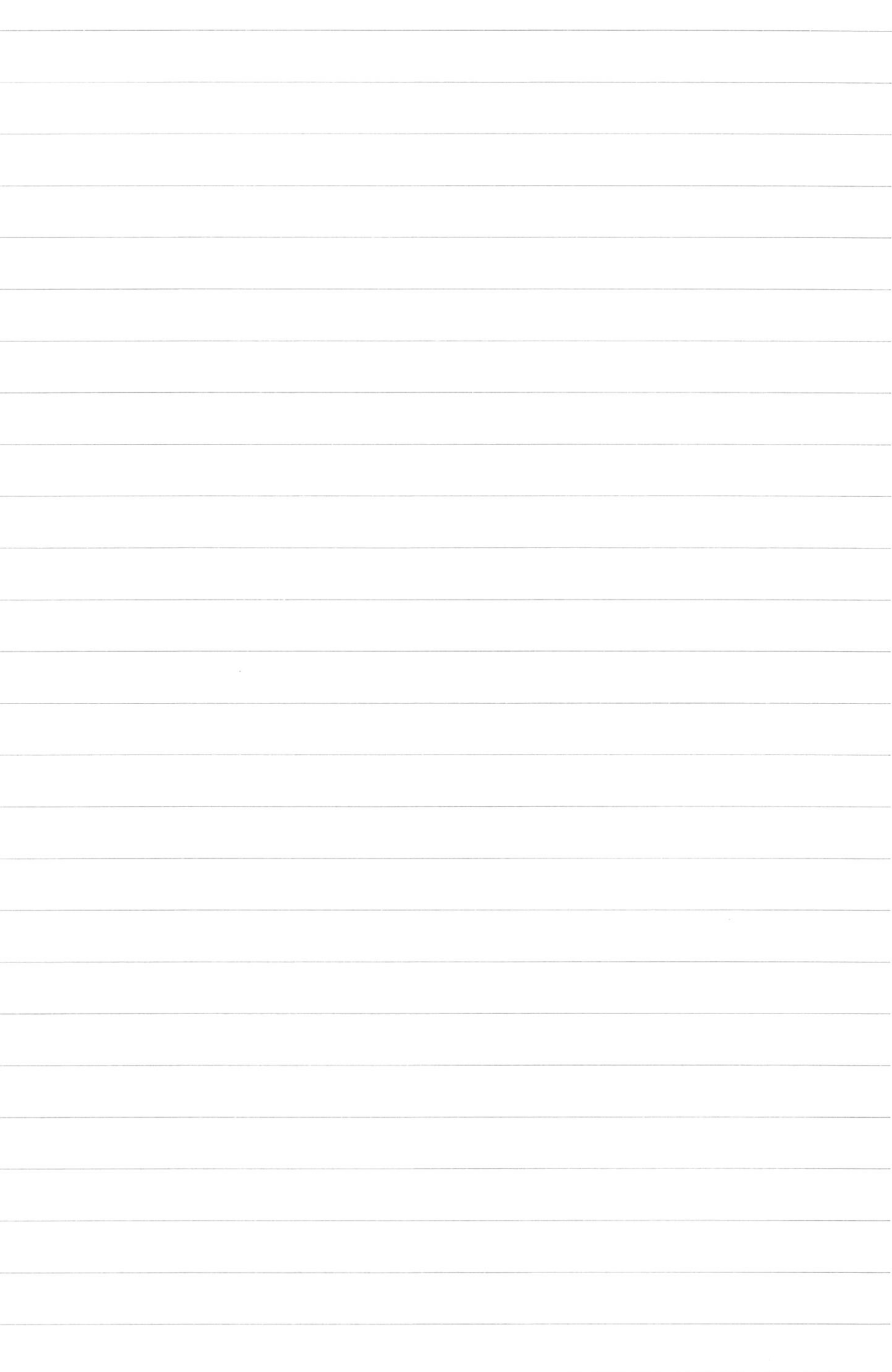

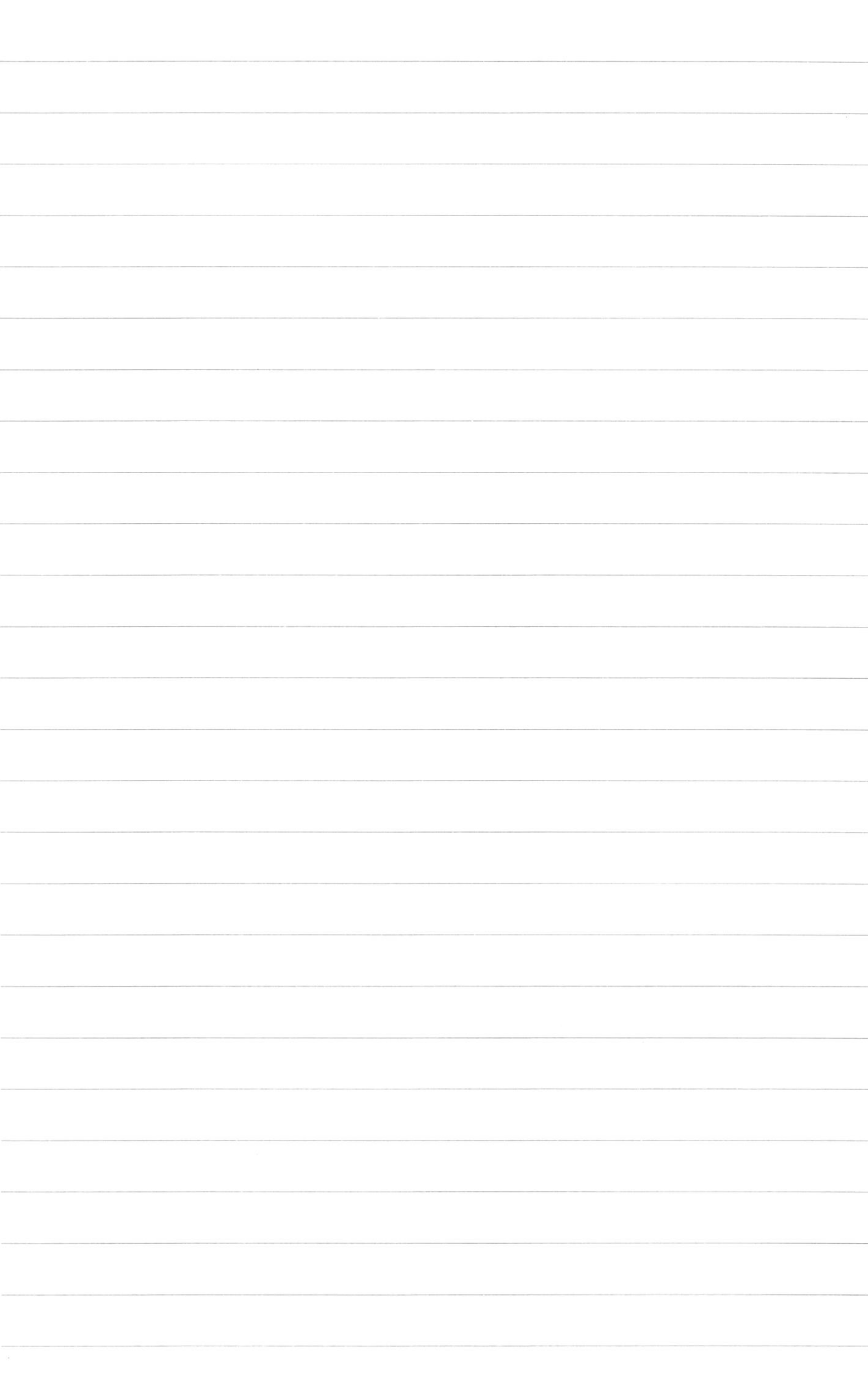

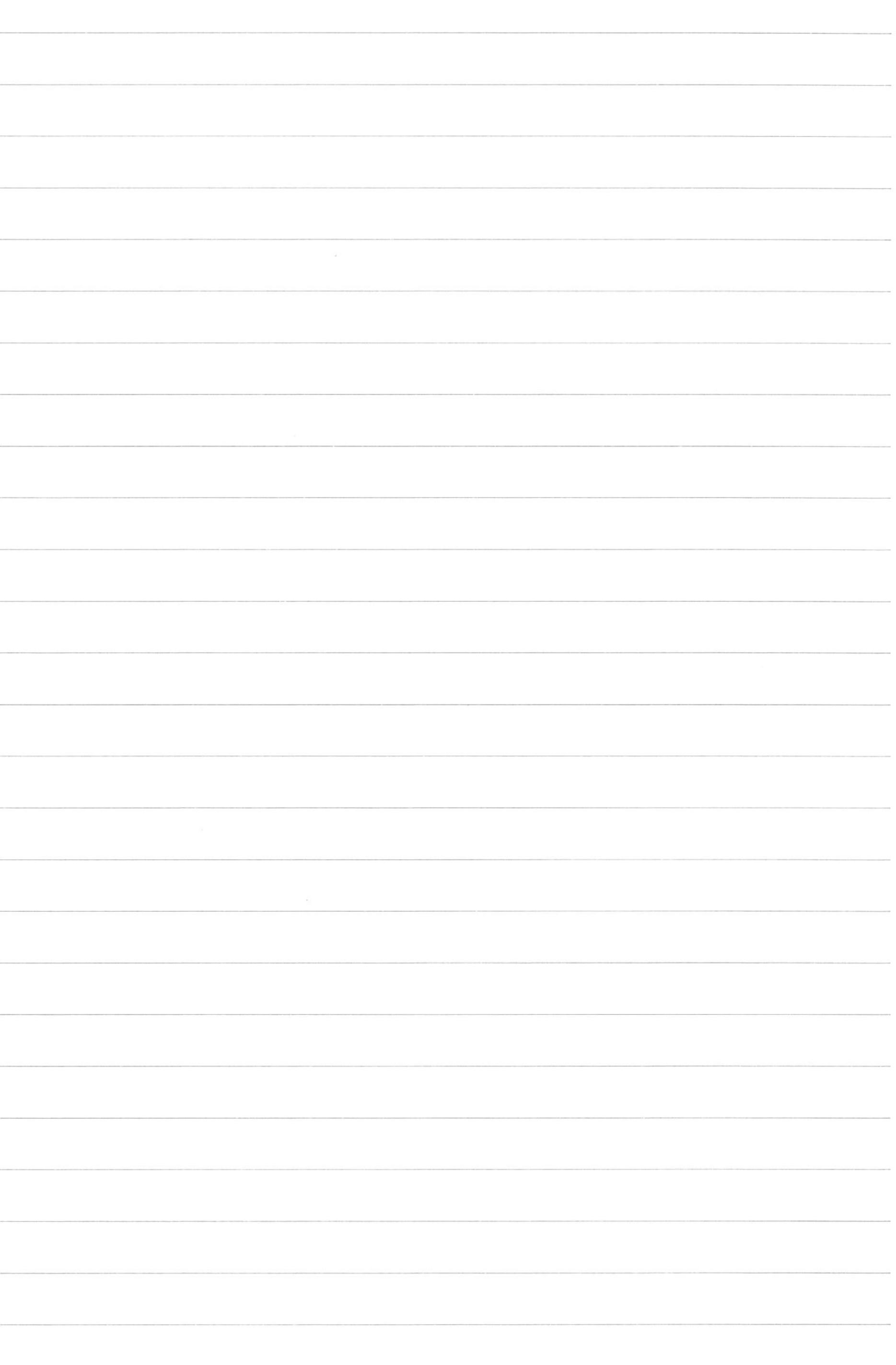

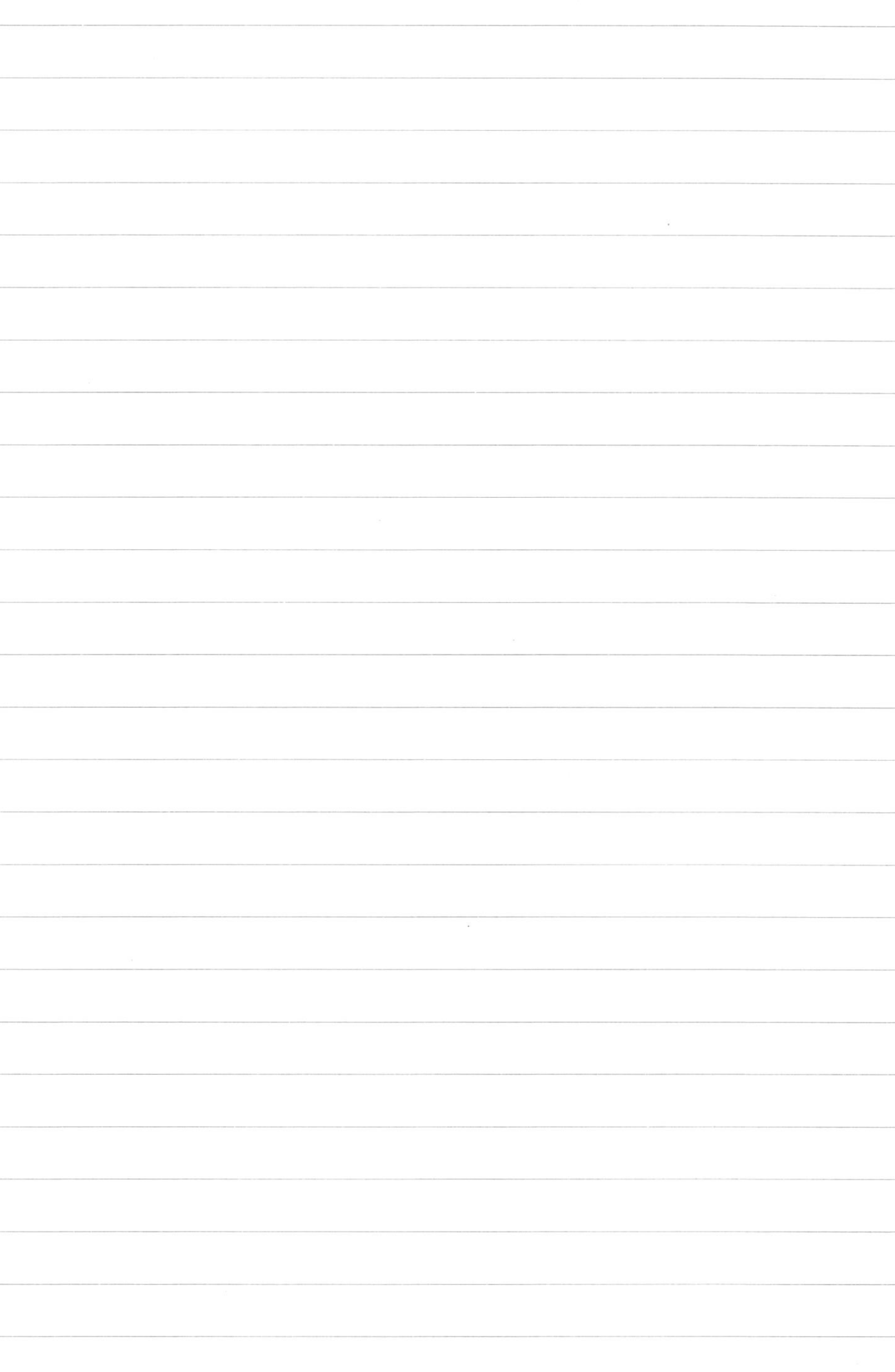

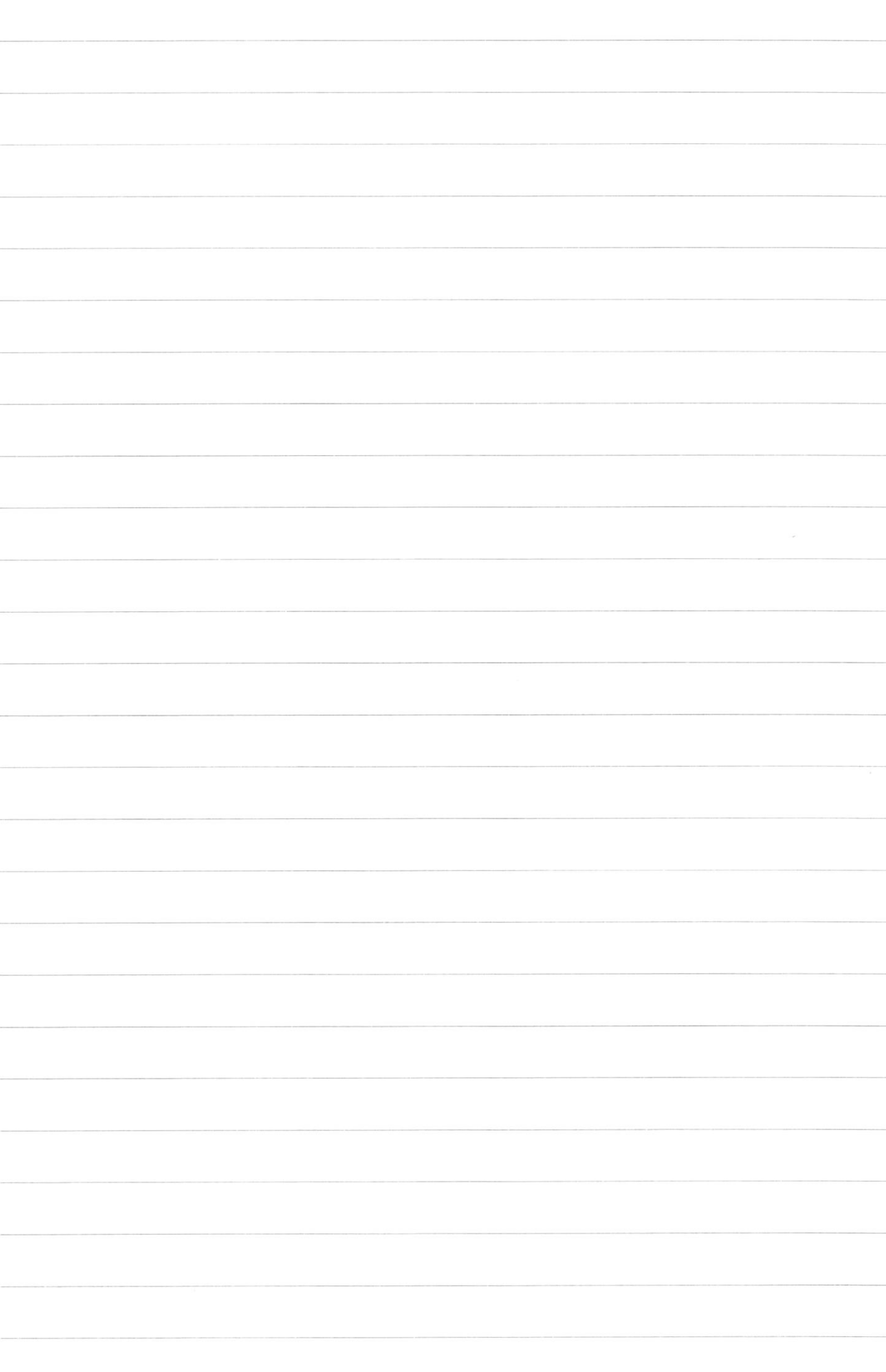

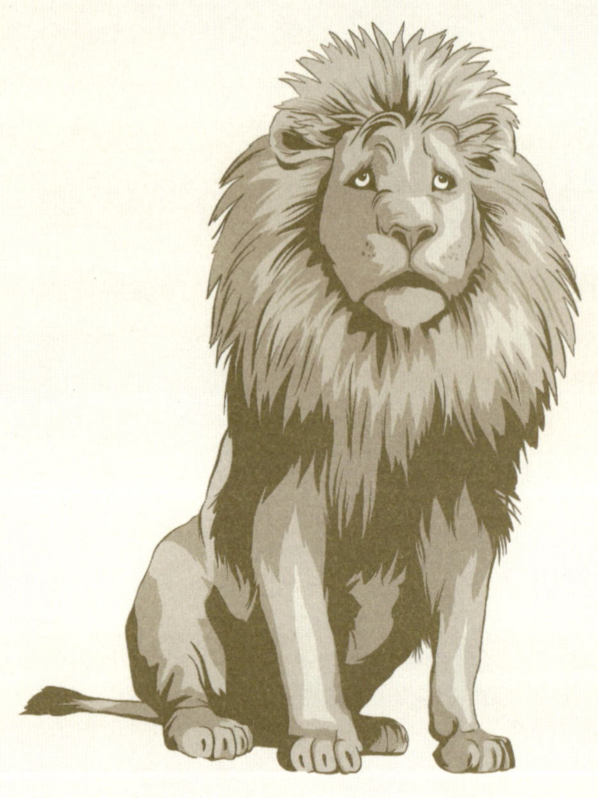

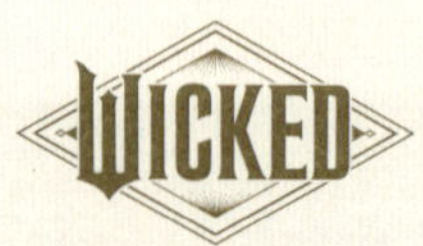

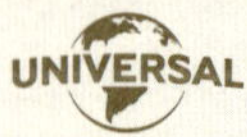

INSIGHTS
insighteditions.com

MANUFACTURED IN VIETNAM

10 9 8 7 6 5 4 3 2 1

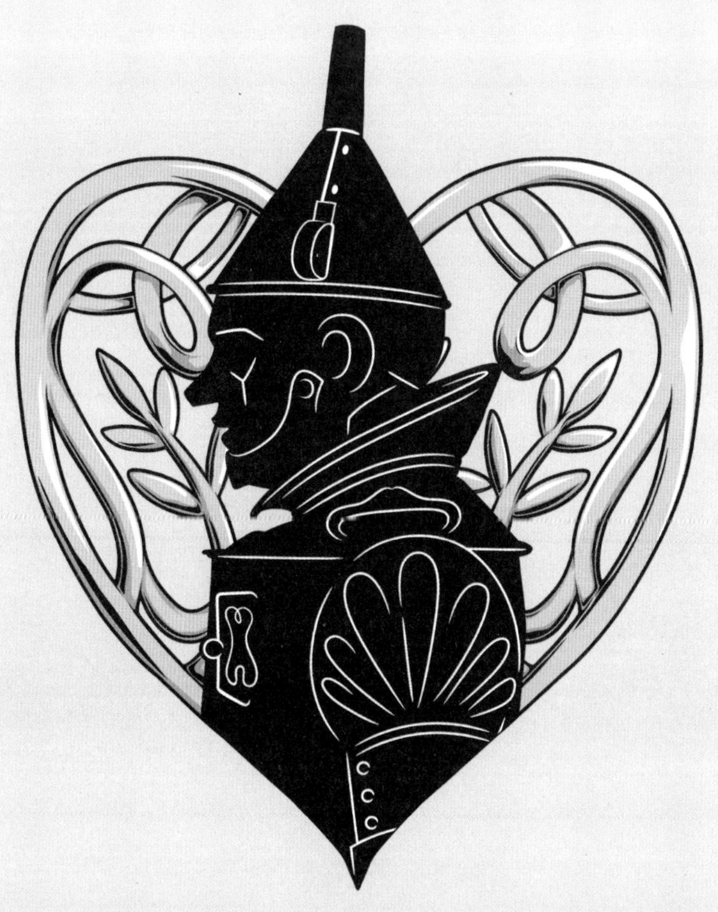

PROPERTY OF

____

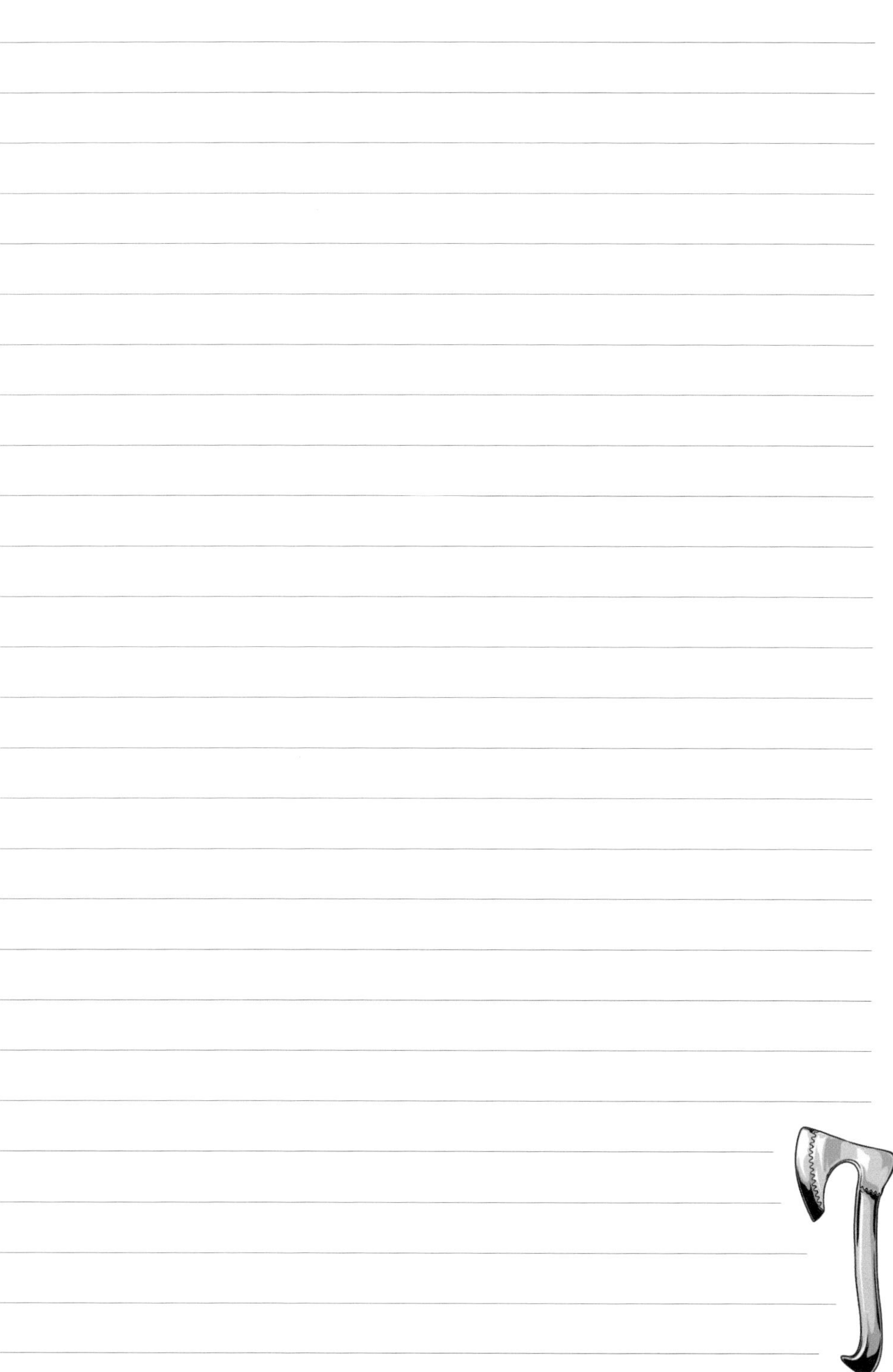

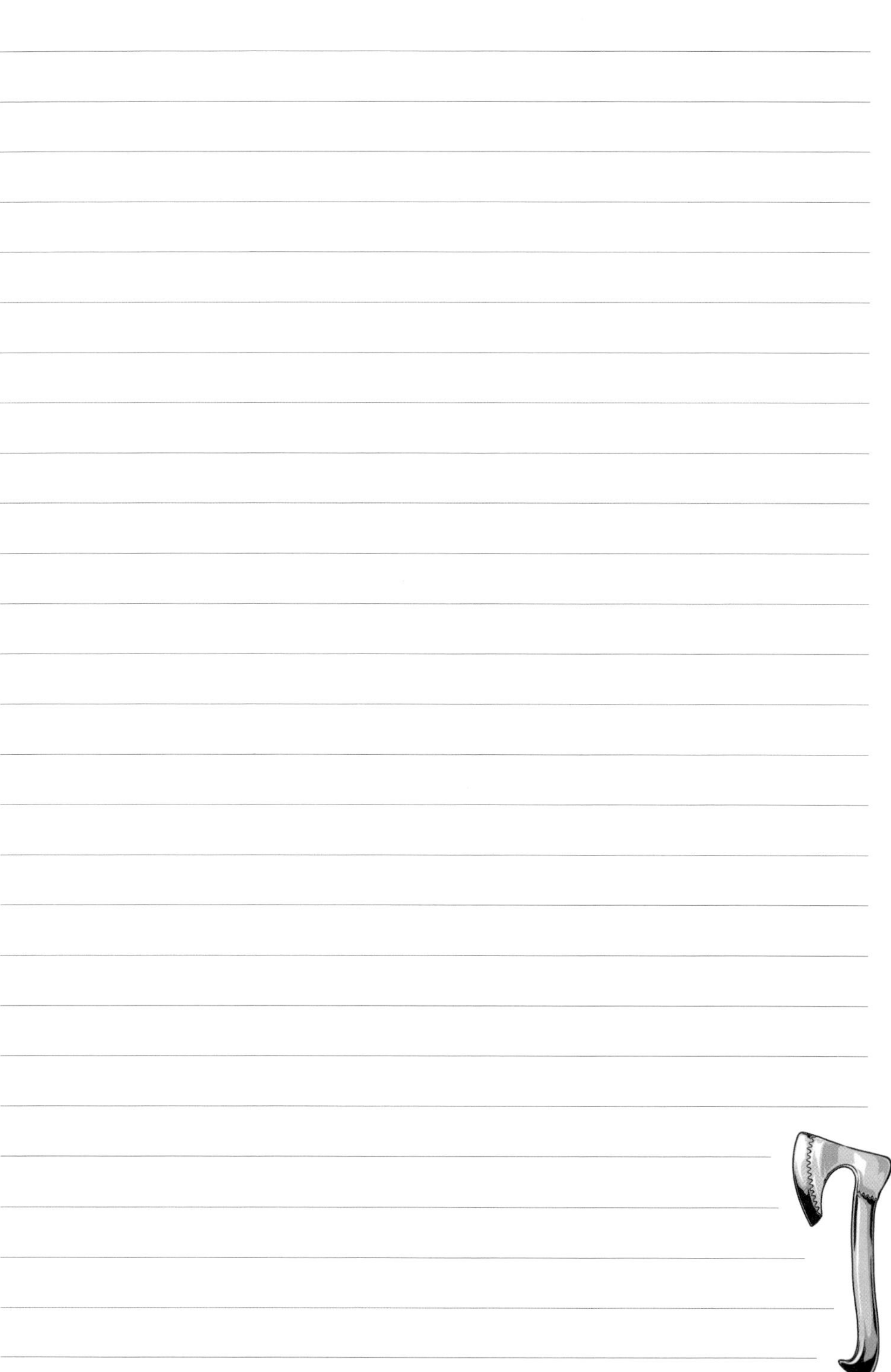

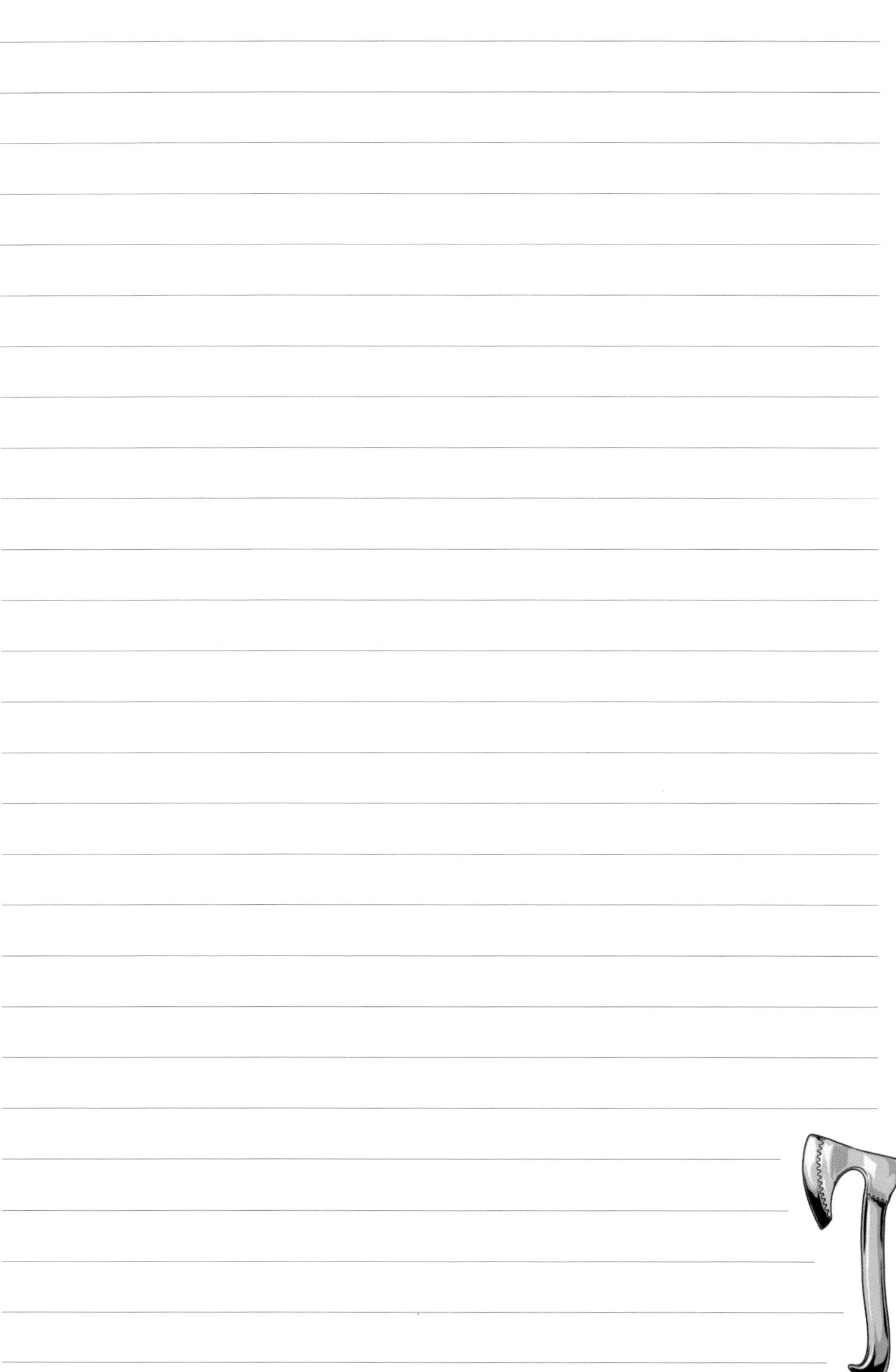

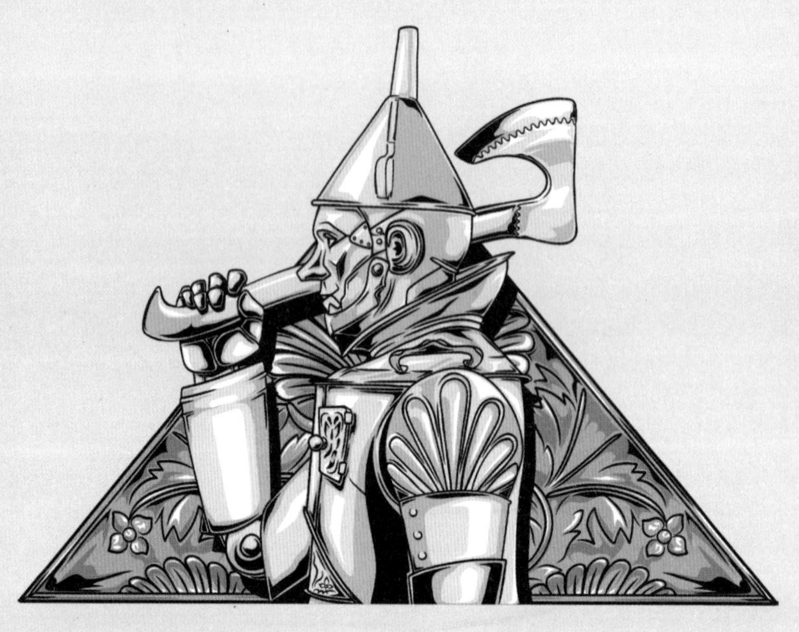

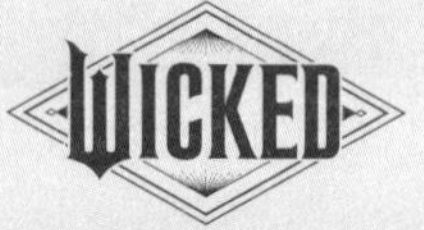

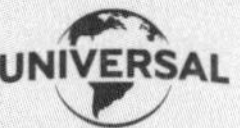

INSIGHTS
insighteditions.com

MANUFACTURED IN VIETNAM

10 9 8 7 6 5 4 3 2 1